Amitiés gourmandes à Nada Day !
Wout Bru 27 /08/2004

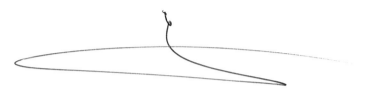

Toujours un plaisir de vous recevoir chez
nous, "CHEZ Bru".
Beaucoup de plaisir avec ce livre !

chezbru

Delicious flavours from Provence

Jean-Pierre Gabriel

STICHTING KUNSTBOEK

Preface

A few summers ago I made a documentary on Provence: 13 episodes with 13 guests. I was paying homage to the region with which I have been in love all my life. We stayed in the loveliest places and, bearing the status of my guests in mind, the culinary level had to be of the highest order. For the episode with Salvatore Adamo, I booked rooms in a medieval alchemist's house, the imposing Mas de la Brune, Eygalières in Provence. Beautiful rooms, an exquisite park, a private swimming-pool… just about everything you need to be perfectly happy - except a chef. 'Breakfast is not a problem but for anything else, you should go to town. A little restaurant recently opened up. Go there; they will look after you splendidly!' Mr and Mrs De Larosière-De Benedetti advised. This golden tip changed my life. What a discovery! Le Bistrot d'Eygalières! And, it so happened that the owners are fellow countrymen. These two young, dynamic Belgians decided to open their temple of dining in the centre of town.

In the meantime, Le Bistrot d'Eygalières has become well known, it has been enlarged and renovated, and it has received official recognition by Le Guide Michelin. Surely, a great many fellow countrymen must have been spoilt by Wout and Suzy over the past few years! Without a doubt, they put Eygalières on the map and the locals will vouch for that. Guests include princess Caroline of Monaco and Queen Beatrix of the Netherlands, who have enjoyed sitting incognito on the terrace in summer. Every moment in Eygalières is a memorable feast; certainly at Wout and Suzy's. Even the French would have to admit it.

I know many people who go out of their way to visit Eygalières when travelling southward. One weekend at Le Bistrot d'Eygalières means more to me than a fortnight at the coast. After all these years, I've come to know the region like the palm of my hand and one can find fine food everywhere. However, Wout stands head and shoulders above the rest. He uses exactly the same fresh regional products as his colleagues but the result on your plate is totally different. He is a thousand times more creative. He has IT. One could say that the magic in his fingers rejuvenates classic dishes. Most of the chefs in the region still follow the traditional approach: true to the spirit but a bit boring and predictable. Decade after decade the same old story, as if time is standing still at Pagnol. Wout injects fresh and new ideas into the old traditions whilst still respecting the past. Undoubtedly, he learnt the tricks of the trade from the renowned chefs in the area but he has added much of his own touch style. He deserves the result. The dishes are a true reflection of the man, Wout. His dishes are works of art. I often hesitate to start eating. His dishes are not only more appealing but the flavours are more intense than anywhere else. In my eyes, Wout can do magic and he continues to surprise one. Also, his lovely wife is the perfect hostess. After my first visit, I wrote the following in the guestbook: 'Anyone who is familiar with the night sky knows that one star shines brighter than all the others. **chezbru** is, in all respects, THE Pole Star of Provence! Congratulations, and if it were up to me, may the stars pour on you.'

Obviously, I am very happy with this book because a magician who shares his secrets is a master. And who doesn't want to do magic? I do.

Good luck!
Dré Steemans/Felice

Content

chezbru

The foie de canard was sublime, 'better than sex' - Kay Johnson, Wellington NZ Sept. 1997

Once upon a time... many a tale starts with these words as someone looks back in time, even as far back as their childhood, filled with honest memories of parents or a grandmother, born chefs as it were. Once upon a time, in the hotel school of Bruges, two people met in their final year... Suzy studied in the girl's section and Wout with the boys. After four years of specializing in physical education at the secondary school, Wout decided to change to the catering college. He still liked sport but the generic subjects were boring and demotivating. Ever the perceptive psychologist, Father Bru reminded Wout of his childhood. 'Food has always been your passion. Can you still remember how you touched a piece of ham or a fish as if caressing it, as a sign of recognition?'

Later, the boy from Antwerp moved to Bruges, determined to become a chef. After two years, he received his diploma. He was interested in cooking but his teachers foresaw a career 'amongst the clients'. His good looks were to blame; it seemed that fate had determined his destiny.

During his first apprenticeship, his teachers' prediction was about to come true. As Wout wanted to learn French, he decided to do an apprenticeship in Bretagne, close to Lorient, at the Château de Locguénolé, a beautiful house with two ceiling rosettes.

His appearance – which he admitted to paying a lot of attention to – again stood in his way. He went to Bretagne to cook but again ended up 'amongst the clients'. The owners were not very welcoming. The apprentices had to stay in a type of dormitory in the stables of a nearby farm. At night they could hear the cows ruminate on the other side of the wall. The bathroom facilities consisted solely of a washbasin for a quick wash and to rinse your belongings. After work, the apprentices had to drag their tired bodies through the forest on dirt roads to reach their lodgings.

Wout's superior was not the epitome of respect and good conduct. His favorite pastime was to mock the young Belgian's bad French. Wout had to duck more than once to avoid being hit on the head with a plate. He had to make it obvious that he was running the show! His predecessors had left after a day but Wout persisted. He learnt his lessons, and thought of his father's encouraging words predicting a bright future: 'Three and a half months – just hang in there and the time will pass quickly'. During this period Wout had a memorable encounter which made the entire restaurant staff green with envy. The then young Sophie Marceau – who was shooting scenes in the area – complimented him on his beautiful eyes. He promptly turned flaming red.

Back from Bretagne, Wout embarked on his final year of study. Enter Suzy. In preparation of her training in hotel management, she had to follow a year in the boys' section. André, Suzy's father, was rather suspicious of the young man in his daughter's life. Wout was from the east, in the Kempen, north of Antwerp, a far cry from the sober, business-like character of this West Fleming. But André, an expert investor, had his plans in place. A connoisseur of fine food and an expert on good wine, especially grand cru, he decided to buy a beautiful old building and renovate it. It would be the ideal place for his daughter's restaurant one day.

Wout's presence could have thwarted his plans. And, indeed, it did. For his final apprenticeship, Wout answered the call of France yet again, this time, the south where the sun shone brightly. He went to the Lubéron, near Gordes and the region of Sault, in the Mas des Herbes Blanches of Joucas. Suzy found work as an apprentice close by but chose to harvest grapes in Châteauneuf-du-Pape – hard labour for a girl. On their days off, Wout visited her. In Joucas he discovered a different way of cooking, namely with olive oil. Even the staff has a different way of eating. He remembers preparing rabbit with thyme and the long walks he made on behest of the chef. He had a simple task: collecting wild herbs from the region, such as thyme, rosemary, savory and even sage. After graduation, Wout's last apprenticeship led to his first job in Joucas. Wout and Suzy became inseparable and together they learnt 'the trade'. She worked at reception or in the restaurant, and he worked in the kitchen. In Mas des Herbes Blanches they rented a garden house from a chamber maid; this would be their first encounter with snakes and scorpions. But there was a positive side too: the sun, singing crickets and festivals in the many villages of the Luberon, which the young couple visited regularly.

André, a gourmet par excellence, invited them one day to the eminent three-star restaurant of Raymond Thuilier and Jean-André Charial in Provence, l'Oustau de Baumanière. In no uncertain terms, he reinforced the meal at Les Baux-de-Provence with these words: 'This is your calling'. After the season, they returned to Belgium. They offered their services to all the Relais & Châteaux across France. Finally, l'Oustau de Baumanière offered them a job. On 1 April 1987 they started working there. Suzy worked in the restaurant. Wout was disappointed because

he had to work 'down under' in the Cabro d'Or, the annex to l'Oustau. He protested and made known that he would rather have worked in the three-star restaurant. The chef compromised: 'Work in the Cabro for two months and then I'll give you a chance here. Three days, not a day longer'. Two months later he would work in l'Oustau, never to return to the Cabro. He prepared sauces in Baumanière until the end of the season, in November. L'Oustau is THE place to learn the great classic dishes. They are true to the tradition of Escoffier, working with the best products affording a certain luxury. Wout observed and memorized. He remembered the puff pastry, the preparations in a crust, lamb, sea wolf and soup. For the first time, he saw how 'brandade de morue' had to be prepared.

In the fall Jean-André Charial sent the young couple to London. The Auberge Provençale, his restaurant in the St James Court Hotel, was desperate for help. Seeing that Belgians were reputedly good at many languages, Suzy and Wout were considered just the right people for the job.

A year later they would go to London again, after a season in Les Baux. For the first time, Wout worked as chef. He was only 22 but already in charge of nine other chefs. Suzy worked as the hotel's receptionist. Their time in London fills them with only good memories now. Wout developed his own culinary style, with a hint of things to come. Whilst working in Baumanière, he had to limit himself to making sauces but in London he was responsible for everything. The restaurant was Provencal but Wout was Belgian. Consequently, butter and cream were never far away. He infused Provence with Flemish flavors and adorned Belgium with the colors of Provence. He created his 'salade de supoins', his ravioli with pistou served with kidneys with mustard or duck with orange sauce. For the first time he cooked vegetarian.

After all, this was London, an extraordinary city that welcomed all sorts of culinary experiments, in the same category as Sir Terence Conran. Eclectic tastes were also catered for by mystical places such as Bombay Brasserie, the great classic Indian establishment. They spent most of their free time doing window shopping. Basically, going about their business as any other normal young couple would. In addition, there were football matches between the teams of the big hotels: Dorchester, Waterside Inn, Savour, Four Seasons…

When he returned to Baumanière as a seasoned chef, familiar with the pro's and cons of his job, Wout turned out to be an all-round chef. Those who knew him were aware of the fact that 'no' did not exist in his vocabulary. He was jokingly called the 'babysitter of the kitchen' because he spent 17 hours per day in there.

Suzy and Wout knew what they wanted: their own restaurant. Jean-André Charial, who kept in touch with them, offered them the opportunity to run Nord Pinus, an establishment in Arles, whose clients included Cocteau and Picasso. After working in Arles for eight months, another project came up close to Eygalières.

A gardener friend told them about this remote village, next to the 'route départementale 24' which led to nowhere in particular. Eygalières was not on the main routes, such as the highway from Saint-Rémy to Cavaillon. The gardener looked after some of the most beautiful gardens in this village. The inhabitants were discreet and lived in the shadow of the olive trees. Neither Wout nor Suzy had heard of it before. To get an idea of the area, they went to the southern village of Eyguières whose name is very similar.

A grocer's shop was up for sale in Eygalières: a narrow, almost cramped building next to the pharmacy. Wout and Suzy offered to buy the premises. The selling price was reasonable but the additional cost of renovating - fitting a kitchen, adding a cellar and stocking up on good wines - were problematic. Banks in the area were aloof towards the young couple and not willing to lend them the money. The saying goes in Belgium that it is easy to get a loan when you don't need it. Then André stepped in and helped to arrange a loan in Belgium, with real estate as security. In May 1995 the weather changed for the better. Wout and Suzy's restaurant awaited the finishing touches. Only the gable still needed a dab of paint.

A man in shorts strolled by and asked when the restaurant would open to the public. As an aside, he replied 'I'll bring Caroline with me'.

The next day, Thursday, 17 May, a car from Monaco parked under the sycamore trees in the Rue de la République. Caroline of Monaco sat down at a table for five, which her friends had reserved and thus became the first star to visit the bistro in Eygalières. The small area was filled to the brim and would be for the next three weeks after the opening. The grapevine had worked well. In the Alpilles the story went that 'the young chef from Baumanière' had opened a restaurant. The gardener was right. Well protected by the olive groves, in the shade of the vegetation, film stars, television stars, politicians, and sport stars dwell...

Suzy received the guests, Wout cooked in the miniscule kitchen. Their way of receiving clients and the menu did not meet the stringent requirements in order to qualify for a Michelin star. Neither did the name: 'bistro' was misleading. The staff was dressed in long, black aprons, as in a 'brasserie'. The dishes were tasty but sober, as was the crockery; lacking deep plates, 'pure' and no frills.

Why did they choose this? In London Suzy and Wout were seduced by Very Simply Nico, one of the first establishments in the Nico Landenis empire. They liked its style, even more so because Wout did not want to give up one of his pleasures. Once, after hours, he strolled to the cheese trolley with a piece of bread in his hand and made his favorite sandwich, to the great dismay of two inspectors from Gault et Millau who were judging the restaurant. Soon it became clear the Bru had to evolve to meet the needs of clients. They had known him from before and had specific requests. They ordered classic dishes tailor made to their wishes. Wout was totally at home in Provence, where the temperament of his friends, the winemakers, the strong flavor of fresh truffles in January and the taste of the first asparagus determined the atmosphere.

More than ever, influences of the Flemish-Belgian dining culture provided a symbiosis of flavors. While olive oil reigned supreme, butter and cream also made a bow, resulting in a heavenly balance in all dishes. Eighteen months later a surprise awaited him. The 26 year-old Wout was awarded one Michelin star. The

Belgian in Provence was the youngest winner that year. Clients flocked from Marseille, Montpellier and even Paris to the restaurant. Often with one thing in mind: to test the 'youngster' with their specific demands. In 1998 the neighbor, an antiques dealer, wanted to move to another area. He had been living in the adjoining property, and enquired nonchalantly whether 'Le Bistrot' could use some extra space. Thereby the dining area and kitchen could be enlarged. The other floors were extensively renovated; Wout and Suzy had four bedrooms furnished – a stroke of luck for those clients who come from the four corners of the world.

As soon as the first rays of sun appear, clients make a beeline for one of the five tables on the sidewalk. On the gable, next to 'Le Bistrot d'Eygalières', an even more telling name appears, simply chezbru. The interior is devoid of every possible cliché. Provence is the epitome of sobriety and light, two key concepts that typified the area a hundred years or so ago. Only the essentials count, no frills, no excess – such as a pretty table cloth made of white linen set against a light décor of ecru and water green. On the tables light plays with the insignia of Château d'Estoublon – the well-known appellation domain for olive oil from the Vallée des Baux – on the transparent glass oil set.

The dishes look appetizing, appealing and enticing. As a chef, Wout's dishes reflect his fine sense of composition, without losing sight of the value of every ingredient. He likes to combine a wide range of flavors, for instance his caramel sauce on the basis of vinegar. The dishes prepared with puff pastry are master-pieces; these creations are taste revelations caressing the palate.

Complexity does not equal abundance. Cooking means that the authenticity of flavors is respected and preserved. Naturally, sauce plays a role and brings back beautiful memories now and again. Suzy remembers many clients over the years, especially a portly lady in her fifties. Wout had prepared one of the variations on scallops with goose liver pâté. The atmosphere that evening was intimate. Suddenly, a loud voice announced 'this is better than sex', breaking the spell. The appreciation expressed by the lady from New Zeeland has been immortalized in the guest book. Proudly so.

Provence

On maps and in figures Provence stretches over a vast area, from the Côte d'Azur to the Camargue and in the north up to Drôme Provençale. My life revolves around Alpilles and the valley of Les Baux. When I take the road to Le Destet in spring, towards Mausanne, I have the feeling that I belong in this area. The same thing happens when I drive to Aureille and see how the ruins of the castle are etched on the horizon like shadow theatre, and a carpet of olive groves and yellow flowers stretched out before me.

Then there is Mouriès, the largest olive town in France, where the bars are lined up one next to the other. Suzy goes horse riding, leaving Mouriès behind her, as she approaches the Alpilles, together with Dédé and Isa from La Meynaude. They roam majestic landscapes, which cannot be grasped in any other way. It is breathtaking to see how varied the landscape is. Horse and rider: both seem unreal in this realm.

I got to know Provence gradually. When Suzy and I worked in L'Oustau de Baumanière (currently a two-star restaurant in Les Baux), we looked for an excuse on our days off to discover the area. Preferably towards the coast: Cassis, Bandol, Saintes-Maries-de-la-Mer... Because every town had a festival in honour of its patron in summer, we joined in and, naturally, tasted the lovely pastis. There was dancing in all the streets; one still finds so many things here which have disappeared from Belgian cultural life.

In my line of work, I deal with various aspects of Provence every day. Obviously, one finds many vegetables: especially first pickings but also the delicious aroma of ripe summer fruit, such as tomatoes and courgettes. Olive oil could be regarded as the trump card of the region; in such a way that I have changed my dietary habits. Nowadays I eat less meat, for instance.

Provence is also the region par excellence for finding black winter truffles – which I will discuss later in the book. I can assure you: without the unique perfume of the truffle, Provence in your plate will taste distinctly different.

One can write endlessly on the true soul of Provence. Peter Mayle, who lived in the heart of Luberon, knew better than anyone else how to take his characters from their fictional context and make them come to life. I love the freedom bestowed on us by the climate, enabling us to play, unexpectedly, a game of petanque in the shade of the town hall of Eygalières, or to dine with friends, even if I have to cook.

It might sound strange but the morning heat and the blue sky give me, child from the north, the feeling of permanently being on holiday. It's not surprising that Boris, our son, and Lou, our daughter, call themselves 'provençales'.

Candied tomato tart with lavender oil

SERVES 8

24 plum tomatoes
salt, pepper
2 - 3 tablespoons fine
granulated sugar (s2)
olive oil
7 oz (200 g) fresh mozzarella
(fior di latte or buffala)
4 puff pastry sheets, approx.
3.15 x 5.5 inches (8 x 14 cm)
(base recipe, p. 141)

For the lavender oil:
1 sprig fresh lavender
3.4 fluid oz (1 dl)
extra virgin olive oil
gcaramelized balsamic
vinegar (base recipe, p. 138)
basil paste
(base recipe, p. 138)

Peel the tomatoes and halve. Remove the pips and membrane. Arrange the tomatoes on a plate round side up and sprinkle with a little olive oil. Dust with a pinch of sugar, and season with salt and pepper. Caramelize the tomatoes for 3 hours in the oven at 70°C. Cover the puff pastry sheets with a thin layer of mozzarella. Arrange the caramelized tomato halves on top.

For the lavender oil: Remove the flowers from the stems and place in a dish. (Throw away the stems as they taste bitter.) Heat the olive oil in a saucepan. Spoon the oil over the lavender flowers and let them steep for a minute. Strain the mixture immediately.
Trickle lavender oil over the tart. Garnish with a dash of caramelized balsamic vinegar and a drop of basil paste.

The flavor of lavender oil is balanced by adding a bitter aroma, provided by the essential oils.
I prefer straining the oil after a minute, using a cone-shaped sieve. One can prepare a greater quantity of lavender oil and store it in a properly sealed bottle.

Very fruity white wine - young Côtes de Provence

Real 'Soupe au pistou'

SERVES 4-6

4.2 cups (1 l) oxtail consommé
(base recipe, p. 140)
4 gelatin sheets
5.25 oz (150 g) broad beans
5.25 oz (150 g) white beans
5.25 oz (150 g) fine
French beans
1 red pepper
poultry stock
bouquet garni
salt, pepper

Remove the beans, blanch them in salted water and then place in ice-cold water. Remove the skin. Cook the French beans al dente in salted water. Plunge them into ice-cold water. Shell the white beans and cook for 30-45 minutes in the poultry stock, adding the bouquet garni.

Grill the pepper, peel and cut the flesh into diamond shapes. Dissolve the gelatin in cold water and squeeze out. Add the gelatin to the tepid consommé (approx. 35°C/ 95°F) and stir. Arrange the garnishing vegetables on a baking dish and carefully spoon the oxtail consommé over.

Put in a cool place for the consommé to set. Serve this dish cold.

Light, refreshing red wine with fruit - young Côtes du Lubéron

Petits farcis

SERVES 6

For the stuffing:
2.2 pounds (1 kg) veal mince
of haunch
1 big tomato
1 pepper
2 zucchinis
1 teaspoon crushed raw garlic
1 sprig fresh thyme
5.25 oz (150 g) Parmesan
cheese
3 egg whites
olive oil, extra virgin
salt, pepper

To be stuffed:
6 medium-sized tomatoes
6 small zucchinis
6 small peppers
6 cleaned artichoke hearts

Peel the zucchinis and remove 0.2 inches (5 mm) of flesh. Dice the zucchinis, tomato and peppers (without seeds and membranes). Sauté both vegetables for 30 seconds in 0.8 inches (1 cm) of hot olive oil in a pan. Drain the vegetables on a paper towel. Mix the mince with the pepper and zucchinis, crushed garlic, thyme, Parmesan and egg whites. Season lightly with salt and more with pepper.

Leave the mixture for 10 minutes to shrink until the meat changes color and the moisture has evaporated. Strain the mixture, if necessary, and season again. Fill the small vegetables with the stuffing. Arrange on various oven-proof plates: peppers on one plate, and the tomatoes on another, etc. Pour approximately 1 inch (2 cm) olive oil into each plate. Preheat the oven to 170°C/338°F. Leave the vegetables to simmer for 20-25 minutes.

Test with a sharp knife whether the vegetables and stuffing are cooked.

Remove from the oven and leave to drain on a cooling rack to prevent them from marinating in the oil. You can store them in the refrigerator like this and heat in the oven shortly before serving.

Young, fruity white or rosé wine - Baux-de-Provence

Provencal gazpacho with pistes

SERVES 4

For the gazpacho:
1 medium-sized cucumber
1 red pepper
1 medium-sized onion
10 tomatoes
12 basil leaves
8 tips of mint sprigs
salt, pepper
fine granulated sugar (s2)

For the 'pistes':
36 'pistes'
1 clove garlic
1 teaspoon chopped shallots

2 tablespoons olive oil
extra virgin
basil paste with peanut oil
(base recipe, p. 138)

Mix the vegetables and strain through a fine mesh cone-shaped sieve. Season mixture with salt and pepper. Add a pinch of sugar for a milder flavor. Put the mixture in a cool place.
Clean the 'pistes'. Chop off their heads and remove the cartilage. Wash the squid carefully and pat dry. Season with salt and pepper.
Fry the 'pistes' on both sides for 15 seconds in hot olive oil mixed with 1 teaspoon garlic paste (one clove of garlic, crushed, without a kernel) and 1 teaspoon chopped shallots. Drain the squid on a rack.
Arrange the 'pistes' in a deep dish. Sprinkle with gazpacho. Season with basil paste. Garnish with basil and mint.

'Pistes' are small squid or calamari, with very delicate meat. Depending on their size and the region, they are also called 'chipiro' or 'supion'.

Young rosé wine with sufficient body.

Saddle of lamb and lamb's feet with sage

SERVES 4

1 saddle of sucking lamb (approx. 1.54 pounds or 700 g net)
16 unblemished sage leaves
2 sheets phyllo pastry
1 egg white
4.2 oz (120 g) bulgur wheat
6 candied shallots
candied pepper (see recipe p. 54)
8 tablespoons pine nuts
1 teaspoon balsamic vinegar
8 lamb's feet (base recipe, p. 139)
parsley
garlic
bread crumbs
1 tablespoon chopped shallot
olive oil extra virgin
salt, pepper

Cut the phyllo pastry in 12 rounds with a diameter of 2 inches (5-6 cm). Arrange on a plate and coat one side with beaten egg white, using a brush. Bake 2-3 minutes in the oven until golden.

Roast the pine nuts in a hot non-stick pan till golden brown. Deglaze with a dash of balsamic vinegar and sprinkle with a pinch of salt.

Place the bulgur wheat in a pot with boiling salted water. Bring to the boil again and cook for 5 minutes. Remove the pot from the heat and leave bulgur to swell. Drain.

Divide the de-boned saddle of lamb in four. Fry the pieces in olive oil until nicely browned. Bake in the oven for 1-2 minutes at 180°C/356°F.

Sauté the chopped shallots in a saucepan in a bit of olive oil. Add the meat of the feet (base recipe, p. 139).

Add 4 tablespoons of bread crumbs mixed with a little garlic and parsley. Sprinkle pine nuts over.

Mix the caramelized pepper and shallots with the bulgur wheat. Spoon this mixture in the middle of a plate. Arrange the pieces of meat around it. Make a 'sandwich' with the three feet preparations and the pastry rounds, separating them.

Deglaze the liquid with water, sprinkle finely chopped sage over and leave to thicken.

Pour the sauce over the dish. Garnish every plate with 2-3 fried sage leaves.

Gratin of chard

SERVES 2

1 chard
1 pat of butter
1 tablespoon corn starch
5 fl. oz (1,5 dl) crème fraîche
5 fl. oz (1,5 dl) milk
4 tablespoons grated Gruyère
salt, pepper
lemon juice or vinegar

Clean the chard and remove the leaves one by one. Separate the veins from the leaves. Cut the veins in strips of approximately 1.1 inch (3 cm) in length and 0.6 inches(1,5 cm) wide. Immerse in lemon juice or vinegar to prevent from coloring. Sauté chard in a pan without browning. Sprinkle with corn starch and pour a mixture of equal volumes cream and milk into the pan. Sprinkle with salt and season with pepper. Simmer over a low to medium heat. The veins have to be al dente. Add Gruyère towards the end. Leave for a further 5 minutes over a low heat whilst stirring with a wooden spoon. Once everything is well mixed, season to taste and transfer to an earthenware dish.

In the meantime, blanch the green leaves in salted, boiling water. Plunge it into ice water and cover the leave veins. Place the dish in a pre-heated oven of 180°C/357° F for 4-5 minutes. For a more luxurious variation, replace some leaves with slices of black truffles (preferably black winter truffles). A delicious combination!

Dry, white wine with a light fruit aroma – young Coteaux d'Aix-en-Provence

Tart of grilled eggplant

SERVES 4

1 long eggplant
salt, pepper
olive oil, extra virgin
7 oz (200 g) tomato compote
(base recipe, p. 141)

For the sauce
2 peppers
0.53 oz (15 g) freshly
grated ginger
3.4 fl. oz (1 dl) milk
3.4 fl. oz (1 dl) crème fraîche

For the pepper sauce: dice the flesh of the peppers. Add the ginger. Sauté the mixture in olive oil over medium heat until the peppers are tender and nearly caramelized. Mix equal volumes milk and cream. Add to the peppers. Bring to the boil and leave to simmer for 2 minutes. Mash mixture with a fork and strain through a fine mesh cone-shaped sieve.
Cut the eggplant in slices of 0.4 inches (8-9 mm). Arrange one layer of slices on a large baking plate and sprinkle generously with olive oil. Turn them over. Grill the drenched eggplant on both sides. Turn eggplant 90° to create a pretty grill pattern. Keep the eggplant warm (e.g. in the oven at 80°C/176°F).
Warm the tomato compote slightly (lukewarm). Compose a tart by alternating a slice eggplant (4 in total) with a layer of tomato compote (3 in total).

Spicy red wine with body · Côtes du Rhône, Cairanne, Sablet

Provencal tart with tomatoes and black olives

SERVES 4

1 circle baked puff pastry
(approximately 8 inches/
20 cm diameter)
(base recipe, p. 141)
4 tomatoes
10 black Niçoise olives
2 medium onions
2 tablespoons olive oil,
extra virgin
1 teaspoon fine
granulated sugar (s2)
1 clove garlic
10 basil leaves
1 dash balsamic vinegar
fleur de sel
sea salt
ground pepper

Peel the onions and chop finely. Heat 1 tablespoon olive oil in a thick-bottomed pan. Sauté the onions for 3-4 minutes without browning. Sprinkle with granulated sugar and season with salt and pepper. Leave to simmer for 30 minutes over a low heat, stirring occasionally.

Pre-heat the oven to 200°C/392°F.

Arrange the caramelized onions on the pastry. Sprinkle the chopped basil leaves and garlic over. Slice the unpeeled tomatoes and arrange on the pastry. Leave a border of 0.2 inches (5 mm) and garnish with the Niçoise olives.

Place the dish in the oven and lower heat to 180°C/357°F. Bake 10 minutes.

Sprinkle the tart with a little fleur de sel, a few drops of balsamic vinegar and a generous dash of good quality extra virgin olive oil. Garnish with a sprig of fresh basil.

Spicy red wine with sufficient crispness (syrah grape) - young Saint-Joseph

Eygalières

"In the same way as the Mont Saint-Michel appears to float on the sea, the village of Eygalières seems to be swept away by the murmuring of the olive trees."

It is often said that only someone with a good reason or discipline will drive to Eygalières. Far from any connecting roads, this spot has remained a village, with its two cafés, its church, its school, its two hairdressers and its bakers. A social network exists, which meets the needs of the 800 inhabitants, old and young alike, ranging from a supermarket to medical care. Strangely enough, winter has to descend on Eygalières before the lively spirit of the village starts to surface. When that happens, the Friday market will not offer pottery and souvenirs aimed at tourists anymore; they make way for the essentials only. However, one finds the basics: poultry, fish, a farmer selling goat's cheese, a herbalist and even Alex, the pizza man.

Even before the end of winter, the herdsmen start taking their cattle out to graze. One of them lives just a few hundred meters away, seen from a bird's-eye view. Another one, who can often be found on the outer reaches of the village in the direction of Vallongue, comes from Mollégès. A while later, the sheperds take their sheep to the pastures, only to return in fall... This is no bucolic scene but a reality. At Easter the village comes alive again. On Tuesday a pilgrimage to Chapelle Saint-Sixte takes place on top of a cliff, flanked by cypresses. Only a few families still dress their daughters in the traditional costume of the 'Mireilles'. The paltry few fairground attractions in front of Le Bistrot seem unfitting during this period and in our village. Due to our location, flanked by cafés (the one owned by the PMU is, ironically, called Le Progrès), we

are well and truly part of village life, especially when all the tables on the terrace are taken. We live next to the town hall, from where we have a lovely, picturesque view of the old Eygalières. The historical village is raised above the murmuring of the olive groves, similar to Mont Saint-Michel in Normandy that towers above the sea. Etched against the panorama of rocks, the ruins of a windmill, a tower and a belfry can be seen; elegantly, proudly piercing the sky. Some people claim that it looks like a Provencal nativity scene. In the front I have planted some lavender and a few olive trees. Our harvest of 110 or 132 pounds (50 or 60 kg) Grossane is paltry. We take it to the oil press and return with a ticket, a precious token, which entitles us to approximately two gallons (seven or eight liters) of olive oil from Alpilles. Even more important than the product is the journey to the oil press: a sign that we are accepted here, in the heart of Provence by everyone.

Tuna with soy and mango vinaigrette

SERVES 4

1.1 lb (500 g) tuna filet
1 firm avocado
salt, pepper
olive oil
lemon juice
4 deep-fried basil leaves

Mango vinaigrette:
4 tablespoons mango pulp
2 tablespoons olive oil
1 teaspoon lemon juice
salt, pepper

Soy vinaigrette:
1 egg yolk + 1 egg
salt, pepper
sherry vinegar
1 tablespoon chopped raw garlic
1 teaspoon fine granulated sugar (s2)
few drops of lemon juice
1 teaspoon mustard
1,5 tablespoons soy sauce

Tomato tartare:
7 oz (200 g) tomato cubes
1 tablespoon chopped shallot
1 teaspoon sherry vinegar
2 tablespoons olive oil
salt, pepper

Cut the tuna filet in diamond shapes (1.1 inches/3 cm long). Poach in salted, boiling water for 1 minute. Remove pan from heat. Place tuna pieces in cold water with ice cubes to end cooking process. Pat the tuna dry and cut in cubes (3 per person).

Dice the avocado in cubes of 0.2 inches (5 mm). Season with a dash of lemon juice, olive oil, salt and pepper. Turn carefully. For the mango vinaigrette: mix the mango pulp (prepared with raw, mixed mangos) with olive oil and lemon juice. Season with salt and pepper. Place the mixture in the refrigerator for a while.

For the soy vinaigrette: mix all the ingredients to a form a beige sauce. Mix all the ingredients for the tomato tartare well. Arrange two squares of tomato tartare and one square of avocado cubes on each plate. Place three pieces of tuna on top. Pour the two vinaigrettes over and garnish with a deep-fried basil leave (base recipe, p. 139)

Well-rounded white wine - young Bourgogne, Mâcon villages, Saint-Aubin

Sardine tartlet with candied pepper

SERVES 4

4 thin slices farmer's bread
12 sardines
olive oil, extra virgin
lemon juice
4 level tablespoons black
olive tapenade
(see base recipe, p. 138)
4 tablespoons Provencal
ratatouille
1 big red pepper
fine granulated sugar (s2)

For the sauce:
1 teaspoon dried spice cake
(base recipe, p. 139)
1 pinch of star anis in
powder form
1 pinch of dried juniper
berries in powder form
salt, pepper

Mix the dried spice cake with the star anis, juniper berries, salt and pepper. Add 2-3 tablespoons of olive oil. Cut the bread (0.2 inches/5-6 mm thick) in rectangles, which should be as wide as the length of the sardines. Arrange the bread on a dish and sprinkle with olive oil. Toast the bread under a grill. Turn over on the other side.

Peel the pepper (taken directly from the refrigerator) with a parer. Cut the flesh in strips and arrange on a dish. Season with olive oil, salt, pepper and a pinch of sugar. Grill 10-15 minutes in the oven at 170°C/338°F.

Marinate the sardines in olive oil, lemon juice, salt and pepper. Remove the sardine filets from the bone, starting with the head. Arrange the filets on the bread. First spread the toasted bread with the black olive tapenade and then with the Provencal ratatouille. Place alternate strips of candied pepper and sardine filets on the bread. Arrange on a plate and drizzle with a bit of sauce.

Young rosé with body – Tavel, Bandol

Creamy vegetable soups

SERVES 6

500g shelled peas
1.7 cups (4 dl) crème fraîche
6.8 fl. oz (2 dl) milk
3 sprigs mint
salt, pepper

Peas with mint

Bring the cream, milk and mint leaves to a boil. Add the peas.
Remove the pot from the heat as soon as the mixture starts boiling. Mix and strain, using a fine mesh cone-shaped sieve.
Season with salt and pepper.

Dry, fruity white wine – young Côtes du Lubéron

4 - 5 leeks (white part)
butter
olive oil
pinch of cumin
1.3 cups (3 dl) milk
1.3 cups (3 dl) crème fraîche
salt

Leek with cumin

Sauté the leeks in butter with a dash of olive oil. Sprinkle a
pinch of cumin over. The leeks should not brown. Add milk
and cream. Bring to the boil, mix and strain, using a fine mesh
cone-shaped sieve. Season with salt.

Dry, fruity white wine – young Les Baux-de-Provence

2 red peppers
olive oil
0.35 oz (10 g) ginger
1.7 cups (4 dl) milk
6.8 fl. oz (2 dl) crème fraîche
salt

Pepper soup

Dice the flesh of the peppers and sauté in a mixture of olive
oil and chopped ginger. Brown the peppers lightly. Add milk
and cream. Bring to the boil and leave to simmer for 2
minutes. Mix the soup well and strain, using a fine mesh
cone-shaped sieve. Season with salt.

Light red wine with sufficient crispness – young Les Baux-de-Provence

Prawn tempura
with cold tomato ratatouille

SERVES 4

4 large prawns
4 tablespoons chopped chives
batter for tempura
(base recipe, p. 141)

For the garlic and
soy vinaigrette:
1 clove garlic without kernel
1 tablespoon soy sauce
1 teaspoon sherry vinegar
1 teaspoon lemon juice
1 teaspoon fine granulated
sugar (s2)
salt, pepper
grape seed oil

For the slightly sour
ratatouille:
2 tablespoons finely
chopped onion
2 big tomatoes
1 tablespoon white
wine vinegar
1 tablespoon lemon juice
olive oil, extra virgin
grape seed oil

Remove the skin and the outer layer of the zucchini (approximately 0.2 inches/5 mm). Dice the flesh. Fry zucchini with chopped onion in olive oil until crispy. Peel the tomatoes, remove pips and dice the flesh. Mix the ratatouille vegetables and season with salt, pepper, vinegar and lemon juice. Arrange the ratatouille in a ring in the middle of a plate.

Mix all the ingredients for the vinaigrette, except the oil, and place in an electric mixer bowl. Switch on and slowly add grape seed oil until a thick consistency is reached (approximately 2.4 fl. oz /7-8 cl grape seed oil).

Store mixture in the refrigerator and serve chilled.

Remove the tail of the large prawns. Dip them in the cold tempura batter and deep-fry at 180°C/357° F. Arrange the prawns on the ratatouille and pour a little garlic and soy vinaigrette over. Sprinkle with finely chopped chives.

Young Châteauneuf-du-Pape

Terrine of scallops and oyster tempura

SERVES 4

olive oil, extra virgin
16 scallops
4 unblemished hollow oysters
batter for tempura
(base recipe, p. 141)
deep-fried artichokes
(base recipe, p. 138)
balsamic vinegar

For the sauce:
liquid of 10 hollow oysters
1.05 oz (30 g) fresh
unsalted butter
pepper

For the stuffing:
10 hollow oysters
1 cooked lobster tail
4 tablespoons raw
tomato cubes
4 tablespoons preserved
tomato cubes
(base recipe, p. 138)
1 tablespoon finely
chopped shallot
juice of lemon
2 tablespoons walnut oil
1 tablespoon crustacean sauce
(base recipe, p. 141)
salt, pepper

Remove the 10 oysters from their shell and save the liquid.
Prepare the stuffing. Dice the oysters and lobster. Mix with the
raw and preserved tomatoes and shallot. Season with lemon
juice, oil, salt and pepper. Add the crustacean sauce. Clean the
fresh scallops; remove the coral and wash the 4 oysters.
Pat them dry and cut in thin slices.
Cover the inside of a small roundish oven dish with olive oil,
using a brush. Arrange the slices of scallops in the dish,
covering the sides. Spoon the stuffing into the dish. Cover
with cling wrap and place in the refrigerator for 30 minutes.
Turn the dish upside down on a plate.
Strain the oyster liquid and pour into a saucepan with 2 tablespoons lemon juice. Reduce liquid by half. Season lightly with
salt and pepper. Whip the mixture with butter until frothy.
Dip the 4 oysters in the tempura batter and deep-fry at
180°C/357°F. Arrange them on top of the scallop terrine.
Drizzle with the butter and oyster liquid sauce. Sprinkle with a
few drops of olive oil and balsamic vinegar. Add a few deep-
fried artichokes.

Refined, dry white wine, rich in minerals - Chablis grand cru, 3 - 4 years old.

Olive oil

"To make delicious mash with olive oil, you need fruity oil, which you can still find here."

Olive oil - that is Provence pur sang: from Les Baux to Alpilles the landscape is marked by an orderly succession of olive groves. When the wind howls through the groves, the visitor cannot fail to notice the supernatural silver foliage; neither the grueling life of the olive farmer. The oldest ones still remember the frost on 2 February 1956. It was so cold that the trunks of some olive trees split open. This was a total disaster for Eygalières, since 95% of the olive trees had to be removed: for many this is still a painful memory.

I am always impressed by the determined perseverance of the olive growers who obtain only a few liters of oil from one tree. High up on their ladders, protected against the cold as best as they can (November and December are the harvesting months), they repeat the same, never-ending actions: positioning their nets on the ground, 'combing' every branch; collecting the fallen olives, moving to the next tree and repeating his actions.

It is essential that great care is taken during harvesting to guarantee fruity, extra virgin oil with a fresh flavor. The result is evaluated according to its level of acidity. Fallen olives which have lain on the ground for a few days produce rancid oil with an acid level that is too high (extra virgin oil should not have more than 1g oleic acid per 100g). There are not many oil presses in the area. In Fontvieille, for instance, a village not far from Eygalières, only one of the eight oil presses which still functioned up to the 1950s has been preserved, namely Le Moulin d'Alphonse Daudet. Notwithstanding, there are sufficient presses to deal with various types of oils. The press of Jean-Marie Cornille in Maussane (oil co-operative in the Les Beaux valley) produces very special oil. Before being crushed between the presses, the olives lie in the attic where they mature. This ensures a 'chôm' flavor, reminiscent of rancid butter and overripe fruit.

In Raphelle towards Eyguières, Cravenco – also a co-operative – produces different types of oil. Firstly, the installation operates as a modern, uninterrupted chain of activity. Secondly, the olives are processed immediately after harvesting. This is also the case with Rémi and Valérie Reboul-Schneider from Château d'Estoublon. This explains why their extra virgin oil has the aroma of young fruit. Château d'Estoublon – which will boast its own oil press according to rumor – is the ultimate example of this new production method which results in an extremely refined product that respects the flavor of your ingredients.

Eloi Durbach from Trévallon is in the same line of work and produces a much talked about oil in his traditional oil press. Unfortunately, and to my frustration, he can only produce small quantities. To meet clients' high expectations of my olive oil pasta, these products are indispensable. Every expert will agree that all the charms of oil are revealed in warm dishes. Every mistake is therefore anathema.

Grilled fan of al dente vegetables

SERVES 4

1 small yellow pepper
1 small red pepper
8 asparagus tips
1 fennel root
2 firm plum tomatoes
2 custard marrow
1 zucchini
1 small eggplant
olive oil, extra virgin
2 sprigs thyme
fleur de sel de Camargue
1 dl anchoïade
1 small leaf top of
deep-fried celery
(base recipe, p. 138)

Clean the vegetables. Remove the seeds and membranes and use only the flesh of the peppers. Do not cut the asparagus. Cut the fennel in four, top to bottom. Halve the tomatoes and marrows. Cut the zucchini and eggplant in thin slices.
Marinate the vegetables for 2 hours in a flat dish with about 1 inch (2 cm) olive oil and thyme. Drain on a rack and use the oil later.
Heat the grill to a high temperature. Grill the marinated vegetables on both sides. Turn the vegetables 90°, thus creating a diamond pattern. Garnish with deep-fried celery. Arrange on a plate and sprinkle with fleur de sel de Camargue. Serve with well-seasoned anchoïade.

Fruity structured rosé - Tavel or a young Gigondas

Scallops and asparagus on a skewer en asperges

SERVES 4

12 scallops
12 green asparagus
4 sprigs rosemary
(8 inches/20 cm long)

For the sauce:
2 small tomatoes
runny honey
fresh thyme
3.4 fl. oz (1 dl) olive oil,
extra virgin
lemon juice
salt, pepper
1 teaspoon balsamic vinegar

Peel the tomatoes, remove seeds and dice flesh. Season with salt and pepper and sprinkle thyme leaves over. Heat the oil slightly (lukewarm). Stir the honey into the oil. This mixture has to be poured over the tomatoes at the last minute before serving. Add a few drops of lemon juice.

Take 4 straight, thin rosemary sprigs. Slice one end into a sharp point and remove the leaves, leaving a few on the tip. Cut the woody ends of the asparagus, leaving only the top halve (3-4 inches/8-10 cm). Cook the asparagus al dente in salted, boiling water. Plunge in ice water. Fry the scallops on both sides for 30 seconds in hot olive oil.

Thread the asparagus and scallops alternatively on the rosemary sprig 'skewer' and arrange on a plate. Sprinkle tomato vinaigrette over as well as a few drops of balsamic vinegar.

Aromatic white wine - Condrieu, young, nicely rounded and well structured

Lamb noisettes with fresh goat's cheese

SERVES 4

1.1 – 1.3 lb (500 - 600 g)
lamb filet (8 noisettes
approximately 1 inch/
2 cm thick)
1 roll goat's cheese
(as fresh as possible)
1 tablespoon runny honey
2 tablespoons olive oil,
extra virgin
8 teaspoons black
olive tapenade
(base recipes, p. 138)
8 tablespoons
tomato compote
(base recipes, p. 141)
fine sea salt
ground pepper

Season the noisettes with salt and pepper. Fry on both sides in olive oil – approximately 20-30 seconds on each side. Remove and place on a rack, at room temperature. Heat the oven grill.
Cut the goat's cheese in 8 slices of 0.2 inches/5 mm each. Coat every noisette with 1 teaspoon tapenade and tomato compote. Position a slice of goat's cheese on top and sprinkle with a dash of runny honey.
Grill the noisettes for only 5 minutes and serve the meat still pink.

*Solid, complex red wine rich in refined tannins -
Châteauneuf-du-Pape, 10 years old*

Lukewarm toast with gurnard and tapenade

SERVES 4

4 small gurnards
2 thick slices of farmer's
bread (0.6 inch/1-1,5 cm)
olive oil, extra virgin
4 tablespoons tapenade
(base recipes, p. 138)
0.4 cup (8 cl) anchovy
vinaigrette
(base recipes, p. 138)
pepper

Ask the fishmonger to filet the gurnard. Cut both slices into rectangles measuring 2 x 6 inches/5 x 15 cm. Sprinkle both sides with olive oil. Place bread firmly between two grills and toast until golden brown in the oven at 200°C/392°f. Preferably use bread suited for bruschetta. Leave bread to cool on a rack and spread with tapenade.

In the meantime, fry the gurnard filets on both sides. Season with pepper and arrange two pieces on each toasted slice. Place the toast on a plate and sprinkle with a dash of anchovy vinaigrette.

Use tweezers to remove the small bones from the gurnard.

Dry white wine, rich in minerals with a hint of fruit -
Bandol, 2 years old, light and fruity with a certain power

Mash with olive oil

SERVES 4

2.2 pounds (1 kg) medium-sized potatoes (charlotte, ratte)
1 cup (2,5 dl) olive oil, extra virgin
0.6 cup (150 ml) milk
5.25 oz (150 g) fresh, unsalted butter
sea salt
4 pinches fleur de sel

Peel potatoes of similar size. Plunge in salted water and bring to the boil. Cook for 20-25 minutes.
Drain the potatoes carefully and spoon into in a blender.
Mash the potatoes and place in a warm dish. Fold warm milk and butter into the mash, using a spatula. Season to taste with salt. Add the olive oil gradually whilst stirring. Keep the mash warm, using the au bain-marie method. Garnish the bowl shortly before serving with a dash of olive oil and a pinch of fleur de sel.
Possible taste deviations in olive oil are more prominent in warm dishes such as mash. The choice of olive determines the success of the dish.

Rounded, fruity white wine – young Baux-de-Provence

Turbot with first pickings

SERVES 4

3.5 oz (100 g) (net) fresh white beans
chicken broth
one bouquet garni
salt, pepper
12 wild asparagus
12 tips of green asparagus
4 young carrots
string (French) beans
fennel
olive oil
4 cups (1 l) milk
1 sprig marjoram
1 sprig fresh thyme
1 whole shallot
1 pinch coarse salt
8 pepper corns
1.3 lb (600 g) young
turbot filets

For the sauce:
2 tablespoons shallots
1 pat of butter
1 teaspoon honey
0.6 lb (1,5 dl) chicken broth

Garnish:
1 potato

Boil the white beans in the chicken broth together with the bouquet garni, salt and pepper. Clean the wild asparagus, tips of the green asparagus, carrots and beans. Cut the fennel in strips. Cook al dente in salted, boiling water. Sauté the fennel in olive oil shortly before serving. Season with salt and pepper. Bring the milk to the boil, together with the marjoram, fresh thyme and the whole, peeled shallot to a boil. Leave to steep. Strain and season milk with coarse salt and pepper corns. Poach the fish filets for 10 minutes in the simmering milk.
Arrange the poached turbot on the vegetables.
Fry the chopped shallots in butter for 3-4 minutes. Add honey and leave to brown slightly. Pour chicken broth into mixture and reduce liquid by half. Mix and season with salt and pepper. Cut the potatoes in long, thin fingers. Fry in a bit of olive oil and position next to turbot, on top of wild asparagus.
Sprinkle with sauce and a dash of olive oil.

Refined, powerful wine, nicely rounded with a light woody aroma - Bourgogne, Puligny

Truffle

"It is easy to forget that the black winter truffle from France comes mainly from Provence."

It is still not common knowledge that Provence is the largest producer of black winter truffles in Europe. The quantities sold here exceed those of markets in Périgord, Italy, and even northern Spain.

Just looking at them is sufficient: hundreds and hundreds of pounds of 'rabasses' – the Provencal term – changing hands weekly in Richerenches makes one aware of the cultural value of the 'melano' (Tuber melano-sporum). Our closest neighbor, Vaucluse, has at least five regular markets. Nothing odd about that, but only if one knows that the slopes of Ventoux are regarded as a treasury filled with black diamonds. I discovered the intensive use of truffles on my arrival in Joucas. Later in L'Oustau de Baumanière, this was confirmed. As a result, I tried to unearth the myth and the mystery of the truffle. When I opened Le Bistrot d'Eygalières, I knew what a 'melano', suitable for use in the kitchen, should smell like and how to identify it. But I still had to learn how to buy them.

That was the real challenge. The market closest to Eygalières was in Carpentras which I paid a visit. Every Friday morning approximately 440 pounds of truffles change owners. The 'rabassiers' show interested buyers the raw product, which they are allowed to touch. As every novice knows, one has to learn from one's mistakes. The sellers thought I was a tourist. Granted, seeing that I did not look like a local and my accent did not resemble the local dialect.

Often I would be handed overripe truffles. The worms that ruin the black gold were also well camouflaged. On top of this, I had to learn how to identify the 'Ôbrumale' (*Tuber brumale*). It looks like the real McCoy but the taste....

Nowadays it is easier for me. Le Bistrot has become well known in the region and the 'rabassiers' know that I process large quantities of truffles. Consequently, I now have fixed suppliers who bring their freshest truffles, still covered in soil. Almost every week we get calls from new suppliers who want to introduce themselves.

Obviously, every year is different. The best results are achieved if mild down-pours drench the truffle soil at the end of July. However, it should not rain too much in fall or winter.

Drenched soil spoils the taste of the truffle. The black truffle is without a doubt a magical product, and a source of inspiration for the most refined recipes. I do not like combining them with eggs. Just like the locals, I prefer eating them with lamb's lettuce, a dash of olive oil and ground salt. I adore a thick slice of toasted bread, thinly spread with goose liver pâté, thick slices of truffle, fleur de sel du midi and a dash of olive oil. I feel so privileged that I have easy access to all of these things.

Poached egg with three types of white fish and black winter truffle

SERVES 4

4 eggs
1.2 cups (3 dl) vinegar
(for boiling eggs)
4.2 oz (120 g) cod
4.2 oz (120 g) morue
(salted cod), desalinated
2.1 oz (60 g) smoked haddock
1.8 oz (50 g) onion jam
4 tablespoons truffle pieces
(or slices of truffle)
1 slice Basque ham
(0.08 inches/2 mm thick)
cup (12 cl) truffle liquid
2.8 oz (80 g) butter
salt, pepper
0.7 oz (2 cl) sherry vinegar
olive oil, extra virgin

Chop the raw ham finely and fry. Bring 8.5 – 12.6 cups (2 -3 l) water to the boil in a medium-sized pot. Add 1.2 cups (3 dl) vinegar. Break the eggs one by one in a bowl. As soon as the water starts boiling, dip a spatula in and start stirring, to create a small whirlpool. Slip the eggs, one by one, into the whirlpool. Consequently, the egg whites will cling to the yolk. As soon as the egg white sets, remove carefully and place in ice-cold water. Desalt the salted cod by soaking it for 24 hours in cold, running water. If necessary, use a ring to form a tart consisting of three thin layers of fish: raw cod, salted cod and haddock. Put the poached egg on top and place in the basket of a steam cooker. Leave to cook for 3-4 minutes as soon as the water starts boiling. Spoon a heaped tablespoon of onion jam in the middle of every plate. Place the fish tartlet and egg on the onion and remove the ring.

For the sauce, mix the truffle liquid with 1.4 oz (4 cl) water and reduce by half. Add sherry vinegar and reduce by half again. Stir in the butter, season and add ham. Spoon sauce over and around the egg. Garnish with truffle slivers.

Complex white wine. Rounded flavor. - Châteauneuf-du-Pape 5 year

Palette of morel mushrooms with asparagus tips

SERVES 4

30 green asparagus
30 morel mushrooms
2.8 oz (80 g) (net) extra fine
green peas
2 tablespoons port
salt, pepper
1 tablespoon caramelized
balsamic vinegar
(base recipes, p. 138)
3 tablespoons truffle liquid
1 pat of butter

Chop off the woody ends of the asparagus. Plunge asparagus in ice-cold water. Cook in salted boiling water. Drain the water and keep asparagus warm.

Clean the mushrooms, remove the stems and rinse them carefully (3-5 times to remove soil). Leave mushrooms on a tea towel to dry. Fry the mushrooms twice (see base recipe, p. 139) and retain the liquid. Deglaze with port at the end. Keep warm.

Blanche the peas for 2 minutes in salted, boiling water. Keep warm. Leave the liquid of the mushrooms to subside, add caramelized balsamic vinegar and then the truffle liquid. Reduce the mixture and stir in a pat of butter. Season to taste. Blend the sauce in an electric blender.

Arrange all the ingredients on plates and drizzle with sauce.

Powerful, refined red wine. Very aromatic and complex – Hermitage 5 year

Potato broth
with truffle and crispy bacon

SERVES 4

10.5 oz (300 g) Charlotte
potatoes (preferably new)
of equal size
3.4 - 4 cups (8 dl - 1 l) poultry
broth
2.8 oz (80 g) butter
2 tablespoons truffle liquid
4 quail's eggs
2.11 oz (60 g) onion compote
(base recipes, p. 140)
1 tablespoon sherry vinegar
0.4 cup (1 dl) white wine
vinegar (to boil eggs in)
20 unblemished truffle slices
fleur de sel
4 crispy rashers of bacon
(base recipes, p. 138)
salt, pepper

Peel the potatoes. Place in a pot and add the poultry broth and a pinch of salt. Cook for 25-30 minutes. Mash the potatoes in the cooking liquid. Dilute the mixture with some warm broth, if it is too thick. Blend the butter and truffle liquid into the warm mash. Season with salt and pepper.

Warm the onion compote and stir in the sherry vinegar, which will give the compote a sweet and sour flavor. Keep warm. Prepare the quail's eggs in the meantime. Remove the cap carefully with a sharp serrated knife. Bring 4 cups (1 liter) of water and the vinegar to a boil. Stir clockwise with a whisk. Slip the eggs, one by one, into the vortex. This should take about one minute. Remove eggs and place in ice-cold water. Spoon some onion compote into the middle of each plate. Position a poached egg on top. Pour potato broth around the nest. Finish with truffle slices and sprinkle with a little fleur de sel.

Garnish with one rasher crispy bacon.

*Refined, aromatic red wine with supple tannins-
Chambolle-Musigny 10 year or Volnay*

'Tompouce' with pig's feet and truffles from Provence

SERVES 4

1 large potato
8 pig's feet (cooked in broth)
(base recipes, p. 139)
1 teaspoon truffle liquid
2 tablespoons bread crumbs
clove garlic
1 - 2 tablespoons
chopped parsley
salt, pepper
1 oz (30 g) fresh truffle

For the creamy julienne:
2 leeks (white part,
not too thick)
1.8 oz (50 g) goose liver pâté
0.8 cup (2 dl) crème fraîche
salt, pepper
For the sauce:
1 fl. oz (3 cl) truffle liquid
1 tablespoon chopped truffles
0.4 fl. oz (1 cl) water
1 teaspoon sherry vinegar
1 pat fresh, unsalted butter

Prepare the potato chips (base recipes, p. 139). Put the chips in a hot oven one minute before serving. Dry the bread crumbs for 15 minutes in the oven at 100°C/ 212°F. Mix with the parsley and finely chopped garlic. Place the meat of the pig's feet in a non-stick pan. Season with salt and pepper whilst warming up. Add the truffle liquid and bread crumbs, which will mix with the pulpy meat.

Cut the leeks in very thin slices (0.04 – 0.08 inches/1-2 mm) and cook for 10 minutes in the simmering crème fraîche. Season with salt and pepper. Keep warm. Add water and sherry vinegar to the truffle liquid and reduce by half. Whip some butter into the liquid and then stir in grated truffle (e.g. from a tin). Season to taste.

Shortly before serving, stir small cubes of goose liver pâté through the creamy leeks. Distribute over 4 plates. Do the same with one third of the pig's feet. Position a large potato chip on top.

Repeat this action twice. Cover the last layer with fresh, grated truffle and pour some sauce over.

Firm, red wine, strong aroma with supple tannins - Côte-Rôtie 10 year

Lasagna with lobster and Jerusalem artichoke mash with truffle

SERVES 4

14.1 oz (400 g) lobster meat
4 large, fresh pasta sheets
(6 x 6 inches/15 x 15 cm)
salt

*For the Jerusalem
artichoke mash:*
14.1 oz (400 g) (net)
Jerusalem artichoke
3 cups (7 dl) milk
2 tablespoons truffle liquid
truffle oil
6 tablespoons truffle pieces
1 teaspoon fine granulated
sugar (s2)
salt, pepper
1 oz (30 g) Jerusalem artichoke
chips (base recipe, p. 138)
8 tablespoons clarified butter
(base recipe, p. 139)

For the crustacean sauce:
2.7 fl. oz (8 cl) lobster liquid
(base recipe, p. 141)
1 pat of butter
tablespoon honey
piment d'Espelette
strong pepper (cayenne or chili)

Peel the Jerusalem artichoke, put in a pot and pour milk over. Add a pinch of salt. Bring to the boil. Drain the cooked Jerusalem artichoke and squash with a potato masher. Add some truffle liquid, a bit of truffle oil (or extra virgin olive oil), grated truffle and sugar. Season to taste with salt and pepper. Spoon the mixture into the middle of a deep dish.

Cook the pasta al dente in a large pot with salted water. Keep the manufacturer's cooking time in mind.

Divide the lobster meat into 4 portions. Warm in a steam cooker and place on the warm mash together with the Jerusalem artichoke chips. Place one sheet of lasagna on each plate. Keep warm.

Warm the clarified butter and whip until foamy.

Warm the lobster liquid, add honey and season with piment d'Espelette and a pinch of pepper. Add the butter. Season with salt.

Drizzle the lasagna with both sauces.

Grandiose white wine, refined, elegant taste - Bourgogne, Beaune 12 year

Truffle risotto

SERVES 4

2 tablespoons
chopped shallot
olive oil, extra virgin
1.7 fl. oz (5 cl) dry white wine
5 oz (140 g) Italian rice
(carnaroli, arborio,
vialone nano)
3 – 3.4 cups (7 - 8 dl)
chicken broth
4 - 5 tablespoons mascarpone
2.11 oz (60 g) parmesan
2 fl. oz (6 cl) veal stock
0.7 fl. oz (2 cl) truffle liquid
1 dash truffle oil
(or extra virgin olive oil)
1 oz (30 g) truffles
salt, pepper
fleur de sel

Fry the chopped shallot in a large, thick-bottom saucepan in oil but do not brown. Deglaze the translucent shallot with dry white wine. Reduce almost all liquid. Add the rice and stir with a spatula until the rice is warm. Pour the boiling chicken broth over (even a bit more). Season with salt and leave to simmer over a low heat.

Check the rice every 3-4 minutes, adding broth every time. The rice should be ready after 15 minutes. Sprinkle some broth over for the last time and remove from the heat.

Stir mascarpone into the rice with a spatula.

Sprinkle grated parmesan over the rice and whisk the rice to become airy and creamy. Whilst preparing the rice, reduce the veal stock a little. Add the truffle liquid and oil, and season to taste.

Serve rice in a deep, warm bowl. Pour veal stock around edges. Place fresh truffle shavings in the middle. Garnish with a little fleur de sel.

Dry white wine, aromatic, firm and refined - Grandiose wine - Chevalier-Montrachet 5-10 years

Alternative: Firm and refined red wine, lovely rounded flavor and many elegant tannins - Bordeaux Pomerol 15 years

Cream of sea urchin and marinated scallop with truffle

Serves 4

16 scallops
48 sea urchins
1 – 1.4 fl. oz (3 - 4 cl) crème fraîche
1.8 oz (50 g) black winter truffle
salt, pepper
olive oil
fleur de sel
olive oil, extra virgin

For the sauce:
2.7 fl. oz (8 cl) liquid of crab
1 pat of butter

Use a pair of scissors to cut a cap from the top, bottom and in the middle of the urchin. Spoon the orange meat from the urchin with a teaspoon. Rinse any impurities under cold, running water.

Clean the shell of 4 urchins thoroughly.

Keep the meat of 8 sea urchins aside as garnish. Mix the rest of the urchin meat (40) with whipped cream. Season with salt and pepper. Fill the 4 sea urchins with this mixture. Place one urchin in the middle of a plate and garnish with the meat you set aside.

Cut the scallops in thin slices and arrange in a rosette around the sea urchin. Slide a slice of truffle between every second or third scallop. Season to taste with salt and pepper. Garnish every plate with a dash of olive oil and a little fleur de sel.

Heat the crab liquid and whip fresh, unsalted butter into the mixture. Drizzle with sauce.

The sea urchin cream can be refined by adding a spoon of caviar.

Dry white wine, full bodied, rounded and refined. Complex wine – Hermitage 5 year

Lamb's lettuce, parmesan and black truffle clumps

SERVES 4

5.3 oz (150 g) lamb's lettuce
2.11 oz (60 g) parmesan
2.8 oz (80 g) jamón ibérico
(thinly sliced)
2 tablespoons olive oil,
extra virgin
1 teaspoon balsamic vinegar
1.8 oz (50 g) fresh
black truffles
coarse sea salt

Clean and dry the lamb's lettuce thoroughly.

Use a peeler, shaver or cheese knife to cut cheese curls (6-7 curls per person). Cut the ham in thin strips.

Mix lettuce with ham and cheese in a large bowl. Add olive oil and vinegar. Season to taste.

Distribute salad over 4 plates in clumps. Shave truffles thinly. Dress every clump with a single layer of truffle. Brush them with olive oil to cause layers to stick to each other. Sprinkle with a pinch of coarse salt. Garnish with a few lettuce leaves.

Grandiose white wine, nicely rounded, refined with a powerful aroma - Bourgogne, young Meursault 2-3 year

Wine

"We're lucky in that a number of very good producers are active in the
Appellation des Baux-de-Provence, and most of them make biowines."

When you say 'Provence', you think of rosé. We do not want to reinforce this cliché. On the menu at Le Bistrot d'Eygalières, you will find six rosé wines, local and mainly fruity. Naturally, you will also find a selection of Bordeaux in our cellar. However, we focus on the region. But where are the boundaries? In the northern Côtes du Rhône white as well as red wines are produced. Think of Condrieu, de Côte Rôtie, Hermitage. Towards the south, one finds the Côtes du Rhône Village and the fruity Grenache

wines such as Vacqueyras, Gigondas, Rasteau and Cairanne, and then you get the Château-neuf-du-Pape.

Before searching for the iodine in Languedoc, people stop with us. Fortunately, we have a number of excellent producers in the appellation Les Baux-de-Provence, many of whom use biological production methods. In no time, we became good clients of Dominique Hauvette who supplies us with red, white and Chateau d'Estoublon. No one should deny himself the luxury of tasting the great millésimes from Trévallon which do not belong to the appellation any longer. A highlight!

The road south leads to white wines, in all directions: Bellet, Cassis, Palette.

On the subject of red wines, the Languedoc produces real gems. One thing is certain: don't go look for old millésimes because the good bottles of today come from very young domains with equally young vinification.

In order to understand our vision of wine, one would have to spend a year in Le Bistrot d'Eygalières, from March when we open till the beginning of January, the end of our season.

The end of winter, in March, demands full-bodied wines. When spring comes knocking, we find solace in softer red wines, such as an easy drinking Cotes Rotie or a more fruity Grenache wine, in other words Cotes du Rhone Village.

As soon as the sun appears, our guests start drinking aperitifs on the terrace. By the end of May, summer has arrived and olive oil features strongly in all our dishes. People think of only one thing: quenching their thirst. Then the white wines from the coast are brought out, as well as whites from Beaux-de-Provence; a beautiful name which reflects the sun in your glass.

The trend continues from June to mid-September. Our clients often prefer light, fruity wines for lunch. When choosing a red, the Loire is, naturally, most appropriate. In Provence we have fruity rosé wines, such as the Terres Blanches or Mas Sainte Berthe, or in AOC of the Les Baux-de-Provence. Often the choice for dinner is a more classic one. During September mushrooms appear, smelling of humus. This asks for more refined white barrel-fermented (fust) wines or even chardonnay from Bourgogne. November to January is a wonderful period

for the sommelier, for he gets the chance to serve lovely bottles of wine from all over.

Then truffles and game appear. Game asks for red wine from Côtes du Rhône such as the peppery character of the syrah or a Bandol, which develops a nose with aromas of hung game after maturation.

Truffles often surprise. When looking for a red wine, I think of the merlot grape from Pomerol, with its truffle aroma, or even closer to Eygalières, the 'old' Hermitage or Châteauneuf. If we have to bring in a local color, why not change the color? I guarantee that most of my truffle dishes taste delicious with Beaucastel, Clos des Papes and other wines from this legendary appellation.

Anglerfish with bacon and red wine sauce

SERVES 4

1 leek, white part
corn starch
olive oil, extra virgin
1 slice smoked breast bacon
(0.3 inch/8 mm thick)
1.8 pounds (800 g)
anglerfish filets
salt, pepper
4 purple artichokes
1 lemon
5.6 oz (160 g) bacon
3 medium-sized potatoes
2 apples (Golden Delicious)
clarified butter
(base recipe, p. 139)

For the sauce:
1 medium-sized onion
1 pat of butter
1 teaspoon fine granulated
sugar (s2)
1.4 cups (1/3 l) red wine
1 sprig thyme
3.4 fl. oz (1 dl) veal stock
3.4 fl. oz (1 dl) fish stock

Cut the onion in thin slices and fry in butter. Sprinkle sugar over for onions to caramelize slightly. Deglaze with red wine and add thyme. Leave to reduce to 1/5 of original. Add veal stock and fish stock and reduce again to 3/4 of original. Whip liquid into a smooth emulsion by adding a pat of butter. Clean the white part of the leek. Cut in pieces of 2.4 - 2.8 inches (6-7 cm) and slice in thin strips. Sprinkle leeks with corn starch and deep-fry for 1 minute at 180°C/357°F until crispy.
Cut the smoked breast bacon (without rind) in strips of 0.4 inch (1 cm) wide. Stick 4 bacon cubes on each filet by means of an embroidery needle. Season with salt and pepper. Fry the anglerfish on both sides in olive oil. Then bake the fish in the oven for 5-6 minutes at 180°C/357°F.
Clean the artichokes, remove the hard leaves, turn over and remove the choke (hay). Cut the artichoke foundations (hearts) in cubes and place in lemon water (to prevent from coloring). Blanch in salted, boiling water for 3 minutes. Drain and fry the cubes in olive oil for 5-6 minutes. Peel the potatoes. Dice and fry in olive oil for 10 minutes.
Fry the bacon cubes in a non-stick saucepan. Drain on a paper towel. Peel the apples and dice (0.2 inches /5-6 mm). Fry for 2 minutes in clarified butter. Mix all the ingredients and season with salt and pepper. Spoon equal amounts in the middle of each plate. Position anglerfish on top. Garnish with strips of deep-fried leek.

Supple, fruity red wine, refined and light – young Côtes de Provence

Calf's kidneys
with stuffed tomatoes

SERVES 4

4 stuffed tomatoes
(petits farcis, p. 34)
4 kidneys of sucking calf
salt, pepper
3 tablespoons peanut oil
1.7 fl. oz (5 cl) clarified butter
(base recipe, p. 139)
7 oz (200 g) chanterelles
(base recipe, p. 140)

For the sauce:
2 finely chopped shallots
1 sprig thyme
3.4 fl. oz (1 dl) red Port
3.4 fl. oz (1 dl) veal stock
1 pat of butter
salt, pepper

Sauté the shallot with a few fresh thyme leaves. Deglaze with red Port and leave to reduce almost entirely. Add 6.8 fl/ oz (2 dl) veal stock and reduce by half. Season with salt and pepper. Whip some butter in. Season to taste with freshly ground pepper. Remove most of the fat from the kidneys. Leave an uneven edge on the kidneys. Season with salt and pepper. Fry the kidneys in a mixture of peanut oil and fresh, unsalted butter for at least 10 minutes. Baste with the liquid regularly. The kidney is ready when it yields slightly when touched and pink on the inside. If kidneys are harder and firmer, they are medium done. To achieve this, place the kidneys in the oven for 5 minutes at 180ºC/357ºF.

Warm the stuffed tomatoes in the same way.

Clean the chanterelles by brushing them (do not wash in water). Remove the stems (part with soil). Prepare the chanterelles according to the base recipe on page 140.

Leave the kidneys to rest on a cutting board and cut in thin slices (0.1 inch/3 mm).

Arrange slices in a rosette on warmed plates. Place the stuffed tomato in the middle and arrange chanterelles around the tomato.

Firm, red wine, well structured and rich in flavor - Bordeaux Saint-Emilion, 10 year

Pigeon in crispy jacket with candied shallot

SERVES 2

2 pigeons (14 -17.6 oz / 400 - 500 g a piece)
4 candied shallots
olive oil, extra virgin
butter
peanut oil
salt, pepper
8.8 oz (250 g) forest mushrooms
thyme
0.8 cup (20 cl) crème fraîche
4 sheets phyllo pastry
1 egg white
1 oz (30 g) goose liver pâté
0.8 cup (2 dl) poultry stock
1 sprig tarragon
1 pat of butter

Bake the pigeons whole in the oven at 200°C/392°F for 12 -13 minutes, using butter, peanut oil, salt and pepper. Baste them regularly with the cooking liquid. Cut the filets out, de-bone the thighs and keep the meat apart.

Clean the mushrooms and slice. Prepare them according to the base recipe (p. 140). Bring the cream to the boil with a few thyme leaves. Reduce the mixture and add the mushrooms. Leave to reduce even more and drain.

Spread 2 pastry sheets open and brush with a bit of water. Place the filets in the middle, followed by the mushrooms. Position 0.6 oz (15 g) goose liver pâté on them, followed by the thighs.

Make parcels (as with candy) with the 2 other pastry sheets and trim the edges. Bake the parcels in the oven at 200°C/392°F for 8 minutes.

In the meantime, brown the shallots in butter. Place a pastry parcel in each plate and a candied shallot.

To make the sauce, add the tarragon leaves to poultry stock and reduce by half. Strain, using a fine mesh cone-shaped sieve. Whip butter into the mixture. Season to taste.

Refined, firm and elegant red wine - Hermitage, Vosne-Romanée 10 year

Bacon with cabbage and raw goose liver

SERVES 4

20 small round onions
olive oil, extra virgin
4 new potatoes
1 tin goose fat
4 unblemished chard veins
4.2 oz (120 g) Chinese cabbage
4.2 oz (120 g) Savoy cabbage
1.8 oz (50 g) butter
7 oz (200 g) chanterelles
(base recipe, p. 140)
3.5 pounds (1,6 kg) bacon -
4 slices of 14.1 oz (400 g)
(base recipe, p. 138)
2.8 oz (80 g) raw goose liver
salt, pepper
1 teaspoon fine granulated
sugar (s2)
1 teaspoon spice cake crumbs
(base recipe, p. 139)
few wild garden rocket leaves

For the sauce:
caramelized balsamic vinegar
(base recipe, p. 138)
1 pinch of allspice
1 pinch of piment d'Espelette
salt, pepper

Peel the onions and place in a pan. Pour olive oil over. Simmer for at least 1 ½ hours over low heat. Brush the potatoes clean and fry in goose fat for 40-50 minutes over low heat. Clean the chard and blanch in salted water. Plunge in ice-cold water when they are al dente. Choose a few unblemished Savoy cabbage and Chinese cabbage leaves and slice in thin strips. Cook in salted, boiling water for 3 minutes. Drain and plunge in ice-cold water. Afterwards sauté them in butter.
Prepare the chanterelles (base recipe, p. 140). Place the slices of breast bacon (base recipe, p. 138) in a non-stick pan. Fry on both sides. Cut the potatoes (unpeeled) in slices of approximately 1 inch (1,5 - 2 cm) and fry golden brown in olive oil. Position the chard on top, then a thin layer of goose liver and the two types of cabbage and finally the bacon.

Prepare the sauce by heating the caramelized balsamic vinegar and season to taste with herbs and spices.
Fry the onions well and add a pinch of sugar. Warm the chanterelles, and stack on a plate. Drizzle sauce around the bacon. Sprinkle the dish with spice cake crumbs. Garnish with a few garden rocket leaves.

Supple and spicy red wine –Volnay 15 years

Grilled filet of roe-deer with chips and pumpkin mash

SERVES 4

1.3 pounds (600 g) filet of
roe-deer (saddle)
olive oil, extra virgin
butter
8.8 oz (250 g) pumpkin
16 pieces of pumpkin chips
(base recipe, p. 139)
3 - 3.4 cups (7 - 8 dl) milk
5.3 oz (150 g) cleaned
chanterelles
5.6 oz (160 g) raw goose liver
spice cake crumbs
salt, pepper
fleur de sel

For the sauce:
3.4 fl. oz (1 dl) marinade
(base recipe, p. 139)
3.4 fl. oz (1 dl) game stock
1 tablespoon strawberry jam
salt, pepper

Marinade the roe-deer a day in advance (see base recipe, p. 139).

Prepare the sauce. Deglaze the meat with 3.4 fl. oz (1 dl) marinade. Reduce liquid by half. Add 3.4 fl. oz (1 dl) game stock and reduce again by half. Stir in the strawberry jam. Season to taste. Put aside.

Loosen the filets. Season with salt and pepper. Fry the filets for 2 minutes in oil and butter. Place in the oven at 180°C/357°F for 2 minutes. Remove and leave to rest. The meat should be pink.

Cut the pumpkin in chunks. Pour milk over, sprinkle with a pinch of salt and cook for 15 minutes. Mash the pumpkin, using a blender. Season to taste and keep warm au bain-marie. Prepare the chanterelles (see base recipe, p. 140). Fry the 4 pieces of raw goose liver (0.6 inches/1,5 cm thick) on both sides for 1 minute. Sprinkle with spice cake crumbs. Slice the filet and arrange on the pumpkin mash. Place some chanterelles in the middle and the goose liver on top. Garnish with chips and pour a bit of sauce over. Sprinkle with a little fleur de sel and some ground pepper.

Spicy red wine - Côte-Rôtie or Clos de Vougeot 10 year

Wild duck with olives

SERVES 2

1 wild duck of approx. 2.2 pounds (1 kg)
1.4 fl. oz (4 cl) clarified butter (base recipe, p. 139)
2.11 oz (60 g) bacon cubes
7 oz (200 g) red cabbage strips
fresh unsalted butter
1 pinch of brown sugar
1 tablespoon chopped shallots
olive oil
5.3 oz (150 g) chanterelles
6.8 fl. oz (20 cl) duck stock
10 black olives
salt, pepper
8 beetroot chips (base recipe, p. 139)

Remove the skin carefully by scorching it over a flame. Season the duck with salt and pepper and place in a saucepan with clarified butter. Leave to brown on both sides and then bake in the oven at 180°C/357°F for 12 minutes. Remove from oven and cut off the feet and drumsticks. Place in a baking dish again and bake for 5 minutes in the oven. Cover the carcass with aluminum foil and set aside at room temperature.

Fry the bacon cubes in a non-stick pan until slightly brown. Sauté the red cabbage in fresh butter for 7-8 minutes. Add brown sugar, season with salt and pepper and add diced bacon. Sauté the shallots in oil. Prepare the chanterelles (base recipe, p. 140) and save the liquid.

Mix the duck stock with the liquid from the chanterelles and reduce. Whip fresh butter into the mixture and season to taste. Add the olives and leave to warm up. Arrange the cabbage with bacon and then the chanterelles on a plate. Place the duck on top and garnish with beetroot chips. Drizzle with sauce.

One can serve this dish in two courses: first the filet and then the feet and drumsticks.

Hearty, firm red wine - Bordeaux-Saint Julien, Pauillac 10 year

Winter

"People come to the restaurant to eat truffles and game and drink an excellent, full-bodied wine. Every time a feast, a ritual for true gourmands."

The start of the truffle season coincides with the appearance of the first game. Even if you were allowed to hunt earlier, in our climate, you would still yearn for game towards the end of November or beginning of December. Winter has to be knocking on the door. In this region, people associate game with the 'festive period' in its broadest sense - in other words from December to January. People come to the restaurant to eat truffles and game and drink an excellent, full-bodied wine. Every time a feast, a ritual for true gourmands.

As is often the case in the south, those who truly love the good things in life are rather attached to traditional tastes. There is no use in serving meat that has not hung long enough. Small game has to hang for a number of days until the skin starts clinging. Then it is marinated for 24 hours.

During the season, we always have a marinade handy, spicy and seasoned with pepper. Naturally, I could use a classic mix of half white/half red to blend the acid aroma of the red wine but I am lucky enough to get the lees of the red wine from Trévallon - a kind gift from my friend Eloi Durbach.

I only serve young partridge, rabbit and roe. Alas, it is becoming increasingly difficult to find quality game (really in the wild). I have been offered partridges with their gizzards filled with grain. The supplier claimed that the birds feed on the corn fields close to the woods, but that was hard to believe. When purchasing meat one has to be very careful since the client will not be fooled. He will know whether the game on his plate is the real thing or not.

Poultry is roasted on the spit whole, just like saddle of hare. We prepare a stew with the rest of the rabbit. Doe is prepared solely as a filet. For side dishes, I use seasonal fruit and vegetables such as quinces, chard, mushrooms and pumpkin.

My favorite dish, I have to admit, cannot be prepared or served in a restaurant. Only with my hunter friends can I eat it. According to law, only hunters are allowed to shoot snipe and thrush and then consume it immediately. They invite me and we prepare a meal: thrush as a starter and snipe as the main dish. And because all hunters and 'rabassiers' are good friends, they do not begrudge the other anything at a moment like this, least of all an excellent bottle of wine!

Duo of sweetbread and fried goose liver in puff pastry

Serves 4

12.7 oz (360 g) sweetbreads
1 sprig of rosemary
8 pepper corns
4.2 cups (1 l) milk
flour
3 - 4 tablespoons
hazelnut butter
14.1 oz (400 g) raw goose liver
peanut oil
1 tablespoon spice cake crumbs
(base recipe, p. 139)
olive oil, extra virgin
2.9 oz (80 g) candied fig
compote (base recipe, p. 139)
4 potato tarts
8 circles phyllo pastry
with sesame seed
(base recipe, p. 141)
coarse salt
2.11 oz (60 g) rocket leaves

For the sauces:

1 – 1.4 fl. oz (3 - 4 cl) fig vinegar
(base recipe , p. 139)
1.7 fl. oz (5 cl) calf stock
1 pat of butter
3.4 fl. oz (1 dl) poultry broth
3.4 fl. oz (1 dl) crème fraîche
1 tablespoon red Port
0.9 oz (25 g) goose liver mousse
salt, pepper

Place the sweetbreads, rosemary and pepper corns in a saucepan. Pour milk over and bring to a boil. Remove the sweetbreads two minutes after the milk starts boiling; plunge in cold water and remove membranes. Cut in four, dust with flour and fry in butter for 4-5 minutes. Season with salt and pepper. Cut the goose liver in slices of approximately 0.5 inch (1,5 cm). Save a piece for garnishing. Dust the slices with flour. Fry in a dash of peanut oil in a very hot non-stick saucepan. Season with salt and pepper. Fry one minute on a side. Drain on a paper towel. Sprinkle with spice cake crumbs.

Deglaze the saucepan with fig vinegar for the first sauce. Add calf stock and reduce slightly. Whip some butter into the sauce and season to taste. Pour poultry broth into a second saucepan and leave to reduce. Add cream and Port and reduce by half. Add cubes of goose liver mousse. Blend well and season to taste.

Place a slice of goose liver on each plate and spread with fig compote. Place a potato tart on top.

Make a sandwich with two pastry rounds and two raw goose liver curls. Season with coarse salt. Arrange the sweetbreads, rocket and the sandwich on a plate. Drizzle with both sauces.

Firm and aromatic white wine - Meursault 5 - 6 year

Caviar with smoked eel and potato

SERVES 2

3.5 oz (100 g) smoked eel filet
2.11 oz (60 g) caviar
2 unblemished Charlotte
potatoes
2 teaspoons chopped shallots
1.8 oz (50 g) butter
1.4 fl. oz (4 cl) crème fraîche
salt, pepper
1 pinch of piment d'Espelette
1 handful of small
potato chips

For the sauce:
1 teaspoon lemon juice
1 teaspoon wine vinegar
2.7 fl. oz (8 cl) crème fraîche

Clean the potatoes with a brush. Cook in salted water for 20 minutes. Drain and peel while still hot. Mash the potatoes with a fork and add butter and cream to the mixture. Season with salt and pepper; add shallots and piment d'Espelette. Grease a baking ring of 4 inches (10 cm) in diameter and line with the eel filet. Fill with potatoes and arrange caviar on top. Garnish with potato chips.

Prepare the sauce shortly before serving. Mix the cream with vinegar and lemon juice.

Subtle, aromatic champagne - Champagne millésimé - Bâtard-Montrachet

Porcini mushrooms broth with bacon

11.3 oz (320 g) smoked bacon

1 pat of butter

3 tablespoons olive oil, extra virgin

1 – 1.4 fl. oz (3 - 4 cl) cara-melized balsamic vinegar (base recipe, p. 138)

For the cooking broth:

1 carrot

1 onion

1 leek

3.5 oz (100 g) dried white beans

For the porcini mushroom broth:

10.5 oz (300 g) porcini mushrooms

17 fl. oz (5 dl) hearty chicken broth

1 small, finely chopped shallot

1.7 fl. oz (5 cl) cream

1 pinch of piment d'Espelette

Desalt the block of bacon two days before use by leaving it under running water for 24 hours. Place the bacon in 10 ½ cups (2,5 l) of cold water and add the broth vegetables. Bring to a boil and leave to steep over low heat for 12-15 hours. Clean the porcini mushroom and cut in large pieces. Prepare mushrooms according to the guidelines in the base recipe (p. 140). Save the cooking liquid. Add the shallots during the second phase and leave to sweat for some time.

Add the poultry broth and leave to steep for 15-20 minutes. Season to taste. Mix to a fine consistency whilst adding cream. Remove the bacon from the broth and leave to cool. Remove the rind. Cut the bacon in 12 rectangles (0.8 inch /2 cm long and approximately 0.4 inch /1 cm thick). Fry in butter and olive oil (ratio 1:1) until brown. Drizzle caramelized vinegar over the dish. Place in the oven for 4-5 minutes, preheated at 180°C/357°F. Baste the bacon once or twice with the caramelized vinegar whilst in the oven.

Pour the porcini mushroom broth into a warm, deep plate. Arrange 3 pieces of bacon in each plate. Sprinkle dish with a few drops of olive oil.

Elegant red wine with finesse - Chambolle-Musigny, 10 year

Sea bass filet with tomato compote and cream of beans

SERVES 4

1.3 pounds (600 g) (net)
sea bass

coarse salt

salt, pepper

olive oil, extra virgin

7 oz (200 g) (net) white beans

4.2 cups (1 l) poultry broth

1 sprig of thyme

1 sprig of savory

3.4 fl. oz (1 dl) milk

tomato compote
(base recipe, p. 141)

2 teaspoons basil paste
(base recipe, p. 138)

Use a fish knife to remove the skin of the sea bass and place on a bed of coarse salt for 5 minutes. Rinse the fish under running water and put on baking paper in a baking tray.

Place a second baking tray on top of the fish to secure the filets. Bake in the oven at 180°C/357°F for 5 minutes. Remove and set aside on a cooling rack.

Season the filets with salt and pepper. Fry both sides in olive oil. Remove and bake again for 5 minutes in the oven at 180°C/357°F.

Shell the white beans. Blanch the beans in boiling water for 1 minute and then plunge into cold water. Remove the skin and cook the beans in poultry broth with thyme and savory for 1 hour. Add some pepper, mix well and dilute with warm milk. Season to taste with salt. Strain the mixture, using a fine mesh cone-shaped sieve. Put the bean cream in the refrigerator.

Arrange 2 tablespoons of tepid tomato compote and cold bean cream in the middle of each plate. Position the sea bass filet on top and garnish with the dried skin.

Garnish each plate with a dash of olive oil and a bit of basil paste.

Rounded, dry white wine – lovely, young palette of aromas

Millefeuille of goose liver and melon

SERVES 4

1.3 pounds (600 g) raw
goose liver
flour
salt, pepper
2 small melons
3 tablespoons runny honey
1 oz (30 g) spice cake crumbs
(base recipe, p. 139)
24 potato chips
(base recipe, p. 139)

For the sauce:
1 fl. oz (3 cl) juice from melon
1 tablespoon fine granulated
sugar (s2)
1 tablespoon white
wine vinegar
1.4 fl/ oz (4 cl) calf stock
1 pat of butter

Cut the goose liver in 8 slices of approximately ½ inch (1,5 cm). Dust with flour and season. Place the goose liver under the grill, ensuring a diamond pattern on both sides.

Quarter the melon and scoop as many balls as possible from the flesh. Caramelize the balls in a saucepan with honey for 2 minutes. Use half of the balls and place an equal number in all 4 plates. Position a slice of grilled goose liver on the balls and repeat the layers.

Caramelize the melon juice and sugar in a saucepan. Deglaze with vinegar and reduce. Add calf stock, reduce slightly and whip some butter in. Season with salt and pepper. Drizzle the dish with sauce and sprinkle some spice cake crumbs over. Place a few potato chips on the plate.

Hearty and aromatic white wine - Sauternes or a young Châteauneuf-du-Pape

Porcini mushroom tart

SERVES 4

1.5 pounds (700 g) firm caps
of porcini mushroom
3.5 oz (100 g) onion jam
(base recipe, p. 140)
1 tablespoon fine
granulated sugar (s2)
2 tablespoons pistachio nuts
2 tablespoons walnuts
4 rectangular sheets of baked
puff pastry, approximately
2 x 6 inches (15 x 5 cm)
(base recipe, p. 141)

Brush the caps of the mushrooms. Fry whole mushrooms (see base recipe, p. 140). This will take 3-4 minutes. Slice mushrooms (2 inches /5 cm long and 0.2 inches /5 mm thick).
Warm the onion jam and fold in the sugar, pistachio nuts and walnuts. Spread the mixture on the pastry. Slice the mushrooms again (0.16 inches/4 mm thick) and place in a row on the pastry. Season with salt and pepper. Place on a baking tray.
Bake in the oven at 180ºC/357ºF for 5 minutes.
Serve immediately with a season salad.

Powerful but elegant red wine - Châteauneuf-du-Pape 10 year

Goose liver tart
with sweet-sour sauce

SERVES 4

5.3 oz (150 g) fresh goose liver
7 oz (200 g) goose
liver mousse
4 eggs
2.1 cups (0,5 l) crème fraîche
0.7 fl. oz (2 cl) truffle liquid
salt, pepper
butter
4 tablespoons truffle flakes
4 slices Swedish knäckebröd
fresh truffle slivers (julienne)
4 tablespoons caramelized -
balsamic vinegar
(base recipe, p. 138)

Remove membranes and veins of the raw goose liver and mash with a fork. Mince the goose liver mousse. Place the raw liver, mousse, eggs, cream, truffle liquid, salt and pepper in a mixing bowl.

Mix well, season to taste and add the truffle flakes. Pour the mixture in 4 small, greased baking dishes or forms.

Bake au bain-marie for 20 minutes at 180°C/357°F. Turn the tarts over on the lightly grilled knäckebröd. Garnish with truffles slivers. Serve with a salad and neutral vinaigrette. Drizzle caramelized balsamic vinegar over the dish.

Full, soft wine, crisp and aromatic – young Loire (Savennières) or Jurançon

Goose liver snack with dried fruit

SERVES 2

2.11 oz (60 g) dried fruit
(pistachio nuts, walnuts
and raisins)
Madeira and red Port
2 new potatoes
olive oil, extra virgin
1.3 cups (3 dl) poultry broth
2.8 oz (80 g) raw goose liver
salt, pepper
4.5 oz (130 g) chanterelles
(base recipe, p. 140)
4 chive sprigs
2 figs in syrup
(base recipe, p. 139)

For the sauce:
0.7 fl. oz (2 cl) Madeira
0.7 fl. oz (2 cl) red Port
½ sheet gelatin

Prepare the dried fruit 12 hours in advance by chopping it up and marinating it in Madeira and red Port.

Peel 2 medium-sized potatoes and cut in a cylinder shape. Pour olive oil over and cook for 1 hour over medium heat. Save the oil and use to fry shallots or onions in. Slice the potatoes (0.4 inches/1 cm thick).

Reduce the poultry broth by half. Place potatoes in warm broth for 5-10 minutes. Cut the goose liver in slices of 0.4 inches (1 cm) thick. Season with salt and pepper. Brown slightly in a non-stick pan for 1 minute. Deglaze with Madeira and Port. Save this liquid and thicken by stirring in soaked gelatin. Season to taste.

Arrange 2 potato slices on each plate, followed by 2 liver slices. Drizzle with sauce. Garnish with a dash of the fruit marinade. Place a layer of figs in syrup and chanterelles on the plate. Drizzle the whole plate with reduced Madeira and Port. Garnish with chives.

Very fruity champagne, aperitif wine

Cream of water cress with oysters

SERVES 4

24 oysters
2 bunches water cress
2.1 cups (5 dl) crème fraîche
1 pat of butter
5.3 oz (150) g raw goose liver
1 Granny Smith apple
salt, ground pepper

Open the oysters, save the liquid and strain.

Trim the bottom part of the water cress. Rinse the water cress thoroughly. Warm the cream in a small saucepan. Plunge the water cress into the cream as soon as it starts boiling. Cook for 13 minutes. Season with salt. Do not leave to cool but grind mixture to a pulp immediately.

Strain through a fine mesh cone-shaped sieve. Season to taste and add 3 tablespoons of oyster liquid. Stir in fresh, unsalted butter until the liquid becomes smooth and creamy. Pour the warm liquid into bowls. Arrange the oysters carefully in the bowls, followed by the raw liver (cold) cubes (0.2 inches/5 mm). Peel the apple and dice finely. Sprinkle cream with apple cubes and ground pepper.

If you decide to prepare the cream of water cress in advance, store it au bain-marie in ice water, ensuring its appetizing green color.

Dry, aromatic white wine – a young Cassis or Bandol

Base recipes

Anchoïade (Anchovy purée)

3.5 oz (100 g) salted anchovies (tinned), 6.8 fl. oz (2 dl) extra virgin olive oil

Drain the anchovies of excess oil and place in a small saucepan. Add olive oil and leave to steep over low heat for at least 2 hours. The fish has to 'melt'. Blend mixture well and store in a cool place.

Anchovy vinaigrette

1.8 oz (50 g) salted anchovies (tinned), 5 fl. oz (15 cl) extra virgin olive oil, 1 egg, juice of 1 lemon, 1 pinch of white pepper

Blend the anchovies, lemon juice and egg in a food processor. Add the olive oil gradually, drop by drop. Season with pepper.

Basil paste with olive oil

1 basil bunch, 3.4 – 5 fl. oz (1 - 1,5 dl) extra virgin olive oil, salt

Pick the basil leaves from the stems. Place leaves, 3.4 fl. oz (1 dl) oil and salt in a food processor. Blend well. Add more oil, if necessary. Leave the mixture to rest in a cool place. Covered with a layer of olive oil, this paste can be kept for 2 weeks.

Beet and pumpkin chips

Use a peeler or shaver to cut the beetroot in thin slices. Dust the slices with flour and deep-fry for 20 seconds in oil (olive or peanut) at 170°C/338°F. Shave or peel the pumpkin in the same way and deep-fry but do not dust with flour.

Beurre blanc

5 unblemished shallots, sherry vinegar, 1 teaspoon black pepper corns, 2.8 fl. oz (80 g) salted butter, salt, pepper

Chop the shallot fine. Pour a mixture of sherry vinegar and water over (ratio 1:1). Add the crushed pepper corns. Leave the mixture to reduce almost completely over a low heat. Per portion, take 1 tablespoon of this mixture and add 1 teaspoon of water. Blend well with butter. Strain through a fine mesh cone-shaped sieve and season with salt and pepper.

Black olive tapenade

100 g black olives, 10 salted anchovy filets, 0.4 oz (10 g) capers (preferably in brine), 2 teaspoons extra virgin olive oil

Remove the olive pips, drain the anchovies and cut in thin slices. Place the ingredients in a bowl and mix well. Add a bit of olive oil, if necessary. This tapenade can be kept in the refrigerator under a thin layer of olive oil.

Braised shallots

Peel the shallots but leave intact. Place in a baking dish (earthenware or Pyrex) and cover with olive oil. Bake in the oven at 150°C/302°F for 2 hours. Prick with a sharp knife to check if they are cooked. Finally, scale the shallots.

Breast bacon broth

For every kilogram/2.2 pounds of bacon: 1 carrot, 1 big onion, 1 leek

Desalt bacon by leaving in cold, running water for 24 hours. Place bacon in 1 gallon (4 l) cold water and add the vegetables. Bring to a boil. Put the lid on and leave to steep over low heat for 12-15 hours. Remove bacon from liquid and leave to drain. Remove the rind.

Candied tomatoes

2.2 pounds (1 kg) round, firm tomatoes, 2- 3 tablespoons fine granulated sugar (s2), 2- 3 tablespoons extra virgin olive oil

Plunge the in boiling water for 20 seconds. Remove and plunge in ice-cold water. Peel and quarter. Remove seeds by means of a teaspoon. Brush with a bit of oil. Add salt, pepper and some sugar. Place segments on a baking tray, hollow side down. Bake in the oven at 100°C/212°F for 2 hours or at 70°C/158°F for 3 hours.

Caramelized balsamic vinegar

4 tablespoons sugar, 1.7 fl. oz (5 cl) balsamic vinegar, 3.4 fl. oz (1 dl) calf stock, 1 pat of butter, salt, pepper

Heat the sugar in a thick-bottomed saucepan until it starts to become a light caramel mass. Remove immediately from the heat and deglaze with balsamic vinegar. Return saucepan to heat and add the calf stock. Reduce and whip in butter. Season with salt and pepper.

Chips and deep-fried food

To make potato chips, cut the peeled potatoes in slices of 0.04 inches (1 mm), preferably using a peeler.
Rinse and leave in water for 12 hours. Change the water two or three times. Remove and leave to drain. Pat with a towel and deep-fry until golden brown. Drain the chips on a paper towel.

Clarified butter

Professional chefs place fresh, unsalted butter in a temperature controlled room for a number of hours. Amateur chefs prefer to leave the butter to melt slowly. Wait for the milk solids to collect at the bottom of the saucepan. Strain the liquid. Use a coffee filter, for example.

Cooking pig's or lamb's feet

Pig's or lamb's feet (10-12), 2 carrots, 2 onions, 1 leek, 3 sticks of green celery, 1 unblemished sprig of thyme, 1 small sprig of rosemary, salt

Use a flame to scorch the hair from the pig's feet. Place in a pot and cover with cold water. Bring to a boil. Change the water when adding the vegetables and herbs. Season with salt.
Bring to a boil and simmer for 5-6 hours. The meat should fall from the bone. Drain the feet and then remove the skin and all the meat.

Cooking vegetables

Most vegetables are cooked al dente in salted, boiling water. Drain the vegetables afterwards and plunge in water filled with ice cubes.

Crispy bacon or ham pieces

Cover the oven's baking tray with aluminum foil and place a layer of bacon or ham (0.06 inches /1,5 mm thick) on the tray. Cover again with aluminum foil and repeat. Place an oven dish on top, pressing down on the meat.
Bake in a pre-heated oven at 120°C/248°F. It takes approximately 15 minutes for the meat to dry out. Remove from the oven and leave to cool on a rack.

Crispy phyllo pastry

Roll the pastry: depending on the recipe, one sheet or part of it. Brush with egg white. Sprinkle with sesame seeds.
Bake the pastry between 2 metal plates for 2-3 minutes – pressing upon the pastry. Slide the plates into the same slot. Leave the pastry in the oven to brown, depending on the recipe.

Deep-fried basil

Plunge fresh basil in oil (olive or peanut) at 170°C/338°F. Remove the leaves as soon as they become transparent. Leave to drain on a paper towel. Sage or celery leaves can also be deep-fried.

Dried spice cake

Cut 2 pieces of spice cake in thick slices. Place on a baking tray and leave to dry out in the oven at 90°C/194°F for at least 2 hours.
Crumble the cake or grind until fine.

Fig compote

5 very ripe, peeled figs, 1 cup ($\frac{1}{4}$ l) red wine vinegar, 4.4 oz (125 g) fine granulated sugar (s2)

Place the figs, vinegar and sugar in a saucepan. Bring to a boil and then remove the pan from the heat. Leave aside to rest. Place the compote in the refrigerator. The figs can be used as is or liquidized (without liquid – which can be used separately).

Game marinade

For 8.8 – 11 pounds (4-5 kg) game: 3.2 cups (75 cl) red wine, 3.2 cups (75 cl) white wine (Côtes du Rhône Village), 2 unblemished carrots, 2 onions, 1 sprig of thyme, 1 sprig of rosemary, 1 tablespoon juniper berries, 2 tablespoon black pepper corns

Cut the vegetables in thick slices. Pour both wines in a neutral bowl (glass, plastic, stainless steel or glazed earthenware). Add the game (with or without bones), herbs and vegetables. Cover with aluminum foil and leave to rest for at least 24 hours. Turn the game occasionally. I have the privilege to use lees from wines of the Domaine de Trévallon, which give it an extraordinary flavor.

Onion jam

1.1 pound (500 g) onions, extra virgin olive oil, salt, pepper, 1 pinch of fine granulated sugar (s2)

Peel the onion, slice thinly and place in a thick-bottomed saucepan. Fry in olive oil. Add olive oil until onion slices are covered. Leave to brown slowly for 2 hours. Stir occasionally to prevent the pieces from sticking to one another. Season with salt, pepper and sugar.

Oxtail consommé

For a gelatinous consommé: 6.6 – 8.8 pounds (3 - 4 kg) oxtail, 1 carrot, 1 leek, 1 onion, cloves, salt, pepper, 1 bouquet garni

To clarify: 12.3 oz (350 g) veal mince, 1 medium-sized onion, 1 carrot, 1leek, 2 tablespoons tomato paste, 5 egg whites, salt, pepper

Peel the carrot and clean the leek. Chop the vegetables coarsely. Halve the onion and brown under a grill. Place the oxtail in a big pot. Cover with cold water and bring to the boil. Skim the foam after 5 minutes. Change the water. Add the prepared vegetables and the onion (cloves inserted into onion). Bring to the boil and simmer for 4-5 hours. Strain the consommé, using a fine mesh cone-shaped sieve and pour liquid into pot. You should have 8.5–12.7 cups (2-3 l) of liquid.
To clarify the mixture, chop the carrot and leek finely. Mix with the tomato paste and veal mince. Add the egg whites, which have been beaten stiff. Season with salt and pepper.
Mix into the oxtail consommé and beat well. Leave to simmer for 2-3 hours but do not boil. A crust will form on the broth, which has to be broken now and then. Spoon some liquid over the crust to prevent it from drying out.
Strain mixture, using a fine mesh cone-shaped sieve.

Peeling tomatoes

Make a shallow X-shape at the bottom of every tomato. Plunge a few tomatoes in boiling water for 20 seconds. Remove and place in iced water. Remove and peel tomatoes.

Potato tart

1 potato, extra virgin olive oil, butter, salt

Use a knife to cut the potato in a symmetrical cylinder shape. Slice potato in 0.04 inches (1 mm) slivers using a vegetable shaver.
Arrange the slivers in a rosette shape in a cake tin (which can be lined with baking paper). Brush with olive oil. Bake at 190°C/374°F for 6 minutes. Remove cake tin from oven and leave to cool. Fry the potatoes in a mixture of butter and olive oil until golden brown. Sprinkle with salt.

Poultry broth

2 chickens, 1 quartered onion, 1 bouquet garni consisting of 2 bay leaves (bound), 1 leek, 1 carrot

Remove fat from the chickens carefully and place in a pot with 2.6 gallons (10 liters) water. Bring to a boil and skim off foam. Add the bouquet garni and cook for 3-4 hours. Add a bit of water, if necessary. Strain the mixture, pour back into pot and reduce. You can reduce the mixture to 4.2 -8.5 cups (1 or 2 l), depending on how strong you would like it to be.

Preparing mushrooms

Porcini mushrooms, chanterelles, chopped shallots, extra virgin olive oil, salt, pepper

Preparing mushrooms with olive oil consists of two phases. Fry the mushrooms at a high temperature in oil. Remove the mushrooms but save the liquid (you could use it to flavor a sauce). Fry the mushrooms again in the same saucepan with olive oil and add the chopped shallots (1 level teaspoon per person). Season with salt and pepper at the end.

Provencal ratatouille

1 onion, 1 zucchini, 1 small eggplant, 1 pepper, 2 tomatoes, olive oil, salt, pepper

Fry the onion, pepper, zucchini and eggplant separately in olive oil. Mix the vegetables with some tomatoes for a more subtle flavor. Strain, using a fine mesh cone-shaped sieve thus removing the excess oil. Season to taste.

Puff pastry crust

Roll a puff pastry crust of 0.2 inches (5-6 mm). Place between 2 metal plates – pressing upon the pastry. Slide the plates into the same slot. Bake for 10-12 minutes in a pre-heated oven at 180°C/357°F until golden brown. Cut in pieces, as needed.

Reduced balsamic vinegar

1.7 cups (4 dl) ordinary balsamic vinegar, white wine vinegar (optional)

Reduce the balsamic vinegar to a syrupy mass. Pour into a glass jar (preferably with a lid). For the best results, store at room temperature. If the caramel becomes hard (due to being reduced for too long), dilute with a few drops of white wine vinegar.

Seafood sauce (lobster, scampi, crab...)

4 lobster heads (or the same amount of scampi or crab), ½ fennel, 1 carrot, 1onion, 1 leek, 3 tomatoes, 3 sprigs tarragon, 2 fresh tomatoes, extra virgin olive oil, 5 fl. oz (15 cl) pastis, 1 tablespoon honey, 1 teaspoon piment d'Espelette, 1 pinch of strong pepper (e.g. cayenne), salt, pepper

Chop the vegetables in medium-sized cubes. Crush the lobster carcasses. Fry everything in olive oil for 4-5 minutes. Deglaze with pastis and flambé. Pour water 6.3–8.5 cups (1, 5 -2 liters) over. Bring to a boil and simmer for 2 hours. Mix the ingredients well and strain, using a fine mesh cone-shaped sieve. Pour into a saucepan and reduce by three-quarters. Add the honey. Season with salt, pepper and piment d'Espelette. Keep in the refrigerator until needed.

Tempura

2.1 cups (5 dl) water (of which ⅓ ice cubes), 10.6 oz (300 g) white flour, 7 oz (200 g) potato starch, 2.1 cups (5 dl) water, 1 egg

Mix the flour with the potato starch and store in the refrigerator for 2-3 hours.
Mix the water, ice cubes and egg. Add the flour/starch mixture immediately but little by little whilst mixing all the time, until you have the right consistency. Keep the mixture au bain-marie in ice water.
The freshness of the batter determines the success of the dish.

Tomato compote

For 4.4 pounds (2 kg) tomatoes: 1 onion, 2 cloves of garlic (without kernel and sliced), salt, pepper, fine granulated sugar (s2), extra virgin olive oil, 1 small bunch of basil

Remove the seeds and chop up the flesh. Heat some oil in a thick-bottomed saucepan. Sauté the onion and 1 clove of garlic for 3-4 minutes but do not brown. Add tomatoes and simmer 1 ½ hours over low heat until all the vegetable liquid has evaporated. Season with salt and pepper. Add 1 finely chopped, raw garlic clove and chopped basil to the mixture towards the end. Season to taste and add some sugar for a milder taste.

Colofon

Authors
Wout Bru
Jean-Pierre Gabriel

Translation
Ilze Bezuidenhout-Raath

Photographer
Jean-Pierre Gabriel

Coordination
Philippe Degryse

Final editing
Femke De Lameillieure

Layout and photogravure
Graphic Group Van Damme, Oostkamp

Printed by
Graphic Group Van Damme, Oostkamp

Binding
Scheerders-Van Kerchove, Sint-Niklaas

Published by
Stichting Kunstboek
Legeweg 165
B-8020 Oostkamp
Tel.: + 32 (0) 50 46 19 10
Fax: + 32 (0) 50 46 19 18
Mail: stichting_kunstboek@ggvd.com
www.stichtingkunstboek.com

Wout and Suzy Bru wish to thank
Pierre Mouysset and Céline Viany for their in-
volvement and their precious assistance in
selecting wines for this book; Isa and Dédé de la
Meynaude in Mouriès for the many journeys of
discovery on horseback in the Alpilles; and
Eric and Laurence Hannoun for their hospitality.
A big thank you to all the staff members!

Jean-Pierre Gabriel would like to thank Ariane Le
Fort and Florence Kévers for meticulously and
repeatedly proofreading the text.

Le Bistrot d'Eygalières
Wout & Suzy Bru
Rue de la République
F-13810 Eygalières
Tel.: + 33 490 90 60 34
Fax: + 33 490 90 60 37
Website: www.francemarket.com/bistrot
Email: Sbru@club-internet.fr

ISBN: 90-5856-115-1
NUR: 441
D/2003/6407/14